ST(P) MATHEMATICS 3A

Teacher's Notes and Answers

CW00838860

ST(P) MATHEMATICS series:

ST(P) 1A
ST(P) 1B
ST(P) 1A Teacher's Notes and Answers
ST(P) 1B Teacher's Notes and Answers

ST(P) 2A
ST(P) 2B
ST(P) 2A Teacher's Notes and Answers
ST(P) 2B Teacher's Notes and Answers

ST(P) 3A
ST(P) 3B
ST(P) 3A Teacher's Notes and Answers
ST(P) 3B Teacher's Notes and Answers

ST(P) 4A
ST(P) 4B
ST(P) 4A Teacher's Notes and Answers
ST(P) 4B Teacher's Notes and Answers

ST(P) 5A (with answers)
ST(P) 5B (with answers)

ST(P) 5C
ST(P) 5C Copy Masters
ST(P) 5C Teacher's Note and Answers

ST(P) Resource Book

ST(P) Workbooks:
Drawing and Using Curved Graphs
Measuring Instruments
Symmetry and Transformation
Straight Line Graphs

ST(P) MATHEMATICS 3A

Teacher's Notes and Answers

L. Bostock, B.Sc.

S. Chandler, B.Sc.

A. Shepherd, B.Sc.

E. Smith, M.Sc.

Second Edition

Stanley Thornes (Publishers) Ltd

First Published 1985 by:
Stanley Thornes (Publishers) Ltd,
Ellenborough House,
Wellington Street,
CHELTENHAM GL50 1YD

Reprinted 1986, 1987, 1988, 1991
Second edition 1992
Reprinted 1993

British Library Cataloguing in Publication Data
ST(P) mathematics 3A: teachers notes and answers.
  —2nd ed.—(ST(P) mathematics)
  I. Bostock, L.   II. Series
  510.7

  ISBN 0-7487-1343-3

Typeset by Cotswold Typesetting, Gloucester
Printed and bound in Great Britain by Ebenezer Baylis and Son, Worcester

INTRODUCTION

Book 3A is the third of the A books in the ST(P) graded series in mathematics.

The A series attempts to satisfy the needs of pupils progressing through the National Curriculum and aims to prepare them to achieve about Level 7/8 at Key Stage 3 and the highest level at GCSE. We are aware that among these pupils are those who will eventually decide to aim a little lower and these are the pupils we mean when we talk about the less able in this book. Pupils who by now are quite clearly not going to attempt the highest level GCSE papers in mathematics should not be using Book 3A. The parallel B series contains work designed specifically for them.

Book 3A is a large book for two reasons. Firstly, it contains a lot of revision of earlier work: this does not all need to be worked through with all pupils. It is there partly for reference material for those pupils who may want to reinforce their confidence. Secondly, the book covers the start of many topics that are included in Level 10 of the National Curriculum. We feel that the algebraic skills and the geometric knowledge required for Level 10 need to be absorbed over a two or three-year time span. However, it is probably wise to omit some of these topics with the less able.

Questions that are double underlined, e.g. **7.**, should be used cautiously, if at all, with the less able. They are intended to give the brightest pupils some stretching but can easily damage the confidence of the others. Questions which are single underlined, e.g. **7.**, are extra but not harder questions. They can be used for extra practice or later for revision. Even questions that have plain numbers may not all need to be worked by the brightest pupils. Unnecessary repetition can cause boredom.

The text, though adequate, is brief and leaves ample scope for teachers to use their own methods and ideas. For pupils revising on their own, the explanatory text is a useful reminder of the reasons for the methods followed.

The detailed notes that follow in this book are only suggestions. Teachers will have their own ideas on method and order of content.

Some topics in the first edition of Book 3A have been omitted from the second edition. These are mainly uses of arithmetic and they are covered in other books in the series. Also two topics in the first edition have been moved into the new edition of Book 4A. These are the formal treatment of congruent triangles and matrix transformations.

NOTES AND ANSWERS

CHAPTER 1 Making Sure of Arithmetic

This chapter is mainly revision, but the last section is new work. It can be worked through as consolidation of earlier work or parts of it can be used as and when necessary to act as reminders.

EXERCISE 1a
(p. 2)

This exercise, together with Exercises 1b, and 1c, can be used for discussion and provides a useful reminder of basic operations with fractions, before algebraic fractions—Chapter 23.

1. 21	**5.** 6	**9.** 42
2. 18	**6.** 20	**10.** 18
3. 40	**7.** 12	**11.** 24
4. 12	**8.** 60	**12.** 72

13. $1\frac{13}{24}$	**17.** $1\frac{17}{48}$	**21.** $2\frac{1}{5}$
14. $\frac{9}{10}$	**18.** $\frac{11}{12}$	**22.** $\frac{71}{126}$
15. $1\frac{29}{40}$	**19.** $\frac{8}{9}$	**23.** $1\frac{13}{24}$
16. 1	**20.** $1\frac{3}{4}$	**24.** $1\frac{23}{42}$

25. $\frac{13}{36}$	**27.** $\frac{7}{30}$	**29.** $\frac{1}{40}$
26. $\frac{1}{36}$	**28.** $\frac{1}{20}$	**30.** $\frac{5}{18}$

31. $3\frac{29}{40}$	**34.** $3\frac{11}{12}$	**37.** $4\frac{2}{15}$
32. $\frac{7}{18}$	**35.** $4\frac{7}{8}$	**38.** $\frac{1}{8}$
33. $-\frac{9}{40}$	**36.** $\frac{17}{20}$	**39.** $1\frac{1}{12}$

EXERCISE 1b
(p. 4)

1. $\frac{5}{9}$	**4.** $\frac{1}{10}$	**7.** $\frac{4}{7}$
2. $1\frac{1}{3}$	**5.** $\frac{10}{21}$	**8.** 6
3. $1\frac{1}{2}$	**6.** $\frac{3}{10}$	**9.** $\frac{7}{22}$

10. 2	**12.** 3	**14.** $\frac{4}{3}$
11. 3	**13.** $\frac{3}{2}$	**15.** $\frac{8}{7}$

EXERCISE 1c
(p. 5)

1. $\frac{1}{4}$	**4.** $\frac{1}{10}$	**7.** $\frac{1}{100}$
2. 2	**5.** 8	**8.** $\frac{9}{2}$
3. $\frac{5}{2}$	**6.** $\frac{11}{3}$	**9.** $\frac{4}{15}$

10. $1\frac{1}{3}$

11. 2

12. $\frac{5}{8}$

13. $6\frac{1}{4}$

14. $\frac{14}{81}$

15. $\frac{2}{3}$

16. $\frac{12}{49}$

17. $\frac{1}{18}$

18. $4\frac{1}{2}$

19. $\frac{13}{30}$

20. $\frac{69}{112}$

21. $\frac{8}{25}$

22. $2\frac{1}{18}$

23. $5\frac{3}{10}$

24. $\frac{57}{110}$

25. $4\frac{23}{42}$

26. $\frac{7}{20}$

27. $-\frac{1}{2}$

28. $3\frac{7}{12}$

29. $3\frac{3}{140}$

30. $\frac{2}{5}$

31. $\frac{22}{63}$

32. 14

33. 7

34. $\frac{9}{50}$

35. $1\frac{2}{25}$

36. $\frac{1}{14}$

37. $\frac{21}{68}$

38. $1\frac{1}{4}$

39. 2

EXERCISE 1d
(p. 7)

This exercise, together with Exercises 1e, 1f and 1g, revises basic operations with decimals. If recurring decimals were not covered in Book 1A, they can be discussed now.

1. $\frac{7}{20}$

2. $\frac{27}{125}$

3. $\frac{51}{250}$

4. $1\frac{9}{25}$

5. $\frac{3}{100}$

6. $\frac{3}{250}$

7. $\frac{1}{200}$

8. $1\frac{1}{100}$

9. $\frac{11}{100}$

10. $2\frac{1}{20}$

11. $1\frac{13}{125}$

12. $\frac{1}{10\,000}$

13. 0.15

14. 0.125

15. 0.6

16. 0.24

17. 0.0625

18. 0.54

19. 1.75

20. 0.156 25

21. 0.16

22. 0.3125

23. 2.375

24. 0.002

EXERCISE 1e
(p. 9)

1. $0.\dot{3}$

2. $0.\dot{2}$

3. $0.8\dot{3}$

4. $0.0\dot{6}$

5. $0.\dot{1}4285\dot{7}$

6. $0.08\dot{3}$

7. $0.0\dot{9}$

8. $0.0\dot{5}$

9. $0.41\dot{6}$

10. $0.0\dot{7}1428\dot{5}$

11. $0.2\dot{3}$

12. $0.0769\dot{2}\dot{3}$

EXERCISE 1f
(p. 10)

1. 5.01

2. 19.1

3. 6.17

4. 8.8

5. 1.82

6. 26.36

7. 4.832

8. 1.106

9. 0.002 02

10. 3.2

11. 3.3

12. 0.08

13. 1.21

14. 0.49

15. 23.02

16. 0.361

17. 1.83

18. 0.0068

19. 0.96

20. 0.042

21. 0.008

22. 0.01

23. 0.25

24. 0.360 72

25. 3.36

26. 3.355 11

27. 0.000 384

28. 7

29. 0.3

30. 2.7

31. 0.008

32. 0.015

33. 5.9

34. 1

35. 0.02

36. 0.001

37. 0.6   **40.** 129   **43.** 1   **46.** 0.2
38. 7.8   **41.** 11.882   **44.** 2   **47.** 0.4
39. 0.5   **42.** 3.094   **45.** 1.69   **48.** 8.95

EXERCISE 1g
(p. 11)

1. <   **4.** <   **7.** >
2. >   **5.** >   **8.** >
3. <   **6.** >   **9.** >

10. $0.6, \frac{2}{3}, \frac{4}{5}$ **13.** $\frac{5}{7}, 0.75, \frac{7}{9}, 0.875$
11. $0.79, \frac{4}{5}, 0.85$ **14.** $\frac{3}{20}, 0.16, 0.2, \frac{6}{25}$
12. $\frac{1}{5}, \frac{2}{7}, 0.3$ **15.** $1\frac{1}{8}, 1\frac{1}{5}, 1.24, 1.3$

EXERCISE 1h
(p. 12)
This exercise, together with Exercises 1i and 1j, revises the work on positive and negative indices from Book 2A but with harder examples. Fractional indices are covered in Book 4A.

1. 25   **6.** 144   **11.** 325
2. 81   **7.** 1600   **12.** 8010
3. 32   **8.** 864   **13.** 720
4. 125   **9.** 2048   **14.** 1102
5. 64   **10.** 27 783   **15.** 1 100 000

16. 2^7 **19.** 5^4 **22.** 4^9
17. 3^7 **20.** 2^5 **23.** a^5
18. Not possible   **21.** 7^7 **24.** Not possible

25. 2^2 **29.** Not possible   **33.** Not possible
26. 7   **30.** 3^4 **34.** 64
27. Not possible   **31.** 3^3 **35.** 81
28. 4^3 **32.** a^4 **36.** 15625

EXERCISE 1i
(p. 14)

1. $\frac{1}{2}$ **3.** $\frac{1}{5}$ **5.** $\frac{1}{8}$ **7.** $\frac{1}{a}$
2. $\frac{1}{10}$ **4.** $\frac{1}{7}$ **6.** $\frac{1}{4}$ **8.** $\frac{1}{x}$

9. 3   **11.** 4   **13.** 5   **15.** a
10. $1\frac{1}{2}$ **12.** $1\frac{1}{3}$ **14.** $1\frac{1}{4}$ **16.** $\frac{y}{x}$

17. $\frac{1}{8}$ **19.** $\frac{1}{1000}$ **21.** $\frac{1}{32}$ **23.** $\frac{1}{100}$
18. $\frac{1}{25}$ **20.** $\frac{1}{36}$ **22.** $\frac{1}{10000}$ **24.** $\frac{1}{64}$

25. 125   **27.** 32   **29.** 512   **31.** 8
26. 16   **28.** 81   **30.** 10 000   **32.** 36

33. $1\frac{7}{9}$ **35.** $5\frac{1}{16}$ **37.** $5\frac{1}{16}$ **39.** $123\frac{37}{81}$
34. $3\frac{3}{8}$ **36.** $12\frac{1}{4}$ **38.** $2\frac{7}{9}$ **40.** $2\frac{14}{25}$

EXERCISE 1j
(p. 16)

1. 8
2. $6\frac{1}{4}$
3. $\frac{1}{16}$
4. 64
5. 1

6. 1
7. 125
8. $\frac{1}{9}$
9. 16
10. 1

11. $2\frac{10}{27}$
12. $3\frac{1}{2}$
13. 1
14. $2\frac{314}{343}$
15. $\frac{1}{4}$

16. $\frac{64}{125}$
17. $\frac{1}{12}$
18. 729
19. 64
20. 1

EXERCISE 1k
(p. 16)

This revises standard form. For those with scientific calculators, Number 28 explains the notation used, but there is some variety in the display of scientific notation on different calculators.

1. 345
2. 1200
3. 0.0501

4. 0.0047
5. 280
6. 0.73

7. 902 000
8. 0.000 637
9. 8 720 000

10. 2.65×10^2
11. 1.8×10^{-1}
12. 3.02×10^3

13. 1.9×10^{-2}
14. 7.67×10^4
15. 3.9×10^5

16. 8.5×10^{-4}
17. 7×10^3
18. 4×10^{-3}

19. 5.87×10^4
20. 2.6×10^3
21. 4.5×10^5

22. 7×10^{-6}
23. 8×10^{-1}
24. 5.6×10^{-4}

25. 2.4×10^4
26. 3.9×10^7
27. 8×10^{-11}

28. a) 6.25×10^{10}
    c) 6.4×10^{-9}
    b) 6.6049×10^{12}
    d) 4.9×10^{-11}

EXERCISE 1l
(p. 18)

Deals with decimal places and significant figures and should be revised before later work involving use of calculators, in Chapters 18, 19 and 20.

1. a) 2.785
   b) 2.78
2. a) 0.157
   b) 0.157

3. a) 3.209
   b) 3.21
4. a) 0.073
   b) 0.0733

5. a) 0.151
   b) 0.151
6. a) 0.020
   b) 0.0204

7. a) 0.780
   b) 0.780
8. a) 3.299
   b) 3.30

9. a) 254.163
   b) 254
10. a) 0.001
    b) 0.000 926

11. a) 7.820
    b) 7.82
12. a) 0.010
    b) 0.009 64

13. 0.04; 0.0384
14. 60 000; 47 500
15. 0.05; 0.0447

16. 80; 69.8
17. 0.2; 0.216
18. 500 000; 665 000

19. 2; 2.17
20. 0.2; 0.217
21. 9; 8.89

22. 0.0; 0.0688
23. 5; 4.58
24. 6; 5.38

25. 60; 56.0   **29.** 2; 1.74
26. 0.04; 0.0390   **30.** 0.06; 0.0403
27. 80; 69.3   **31.** 0.1; 0.105
28. 0.03; 0.0328

EXERCISE 1m This section introduces the number line and the open and closed circle notation.
(p. 20) For Numbers 1–20 we suggest that the number line is drawn once and the ranges placed below the line. In Numbers 21–40 the pupils are asked to draw a number line for each question—this takes a considerable time if they are drawn accurately and scaled. It is sensible to encourage rough sketches here.

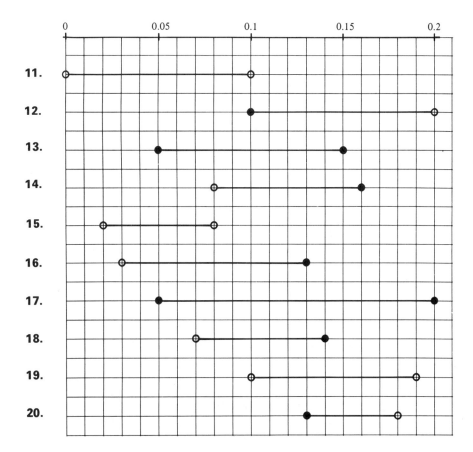

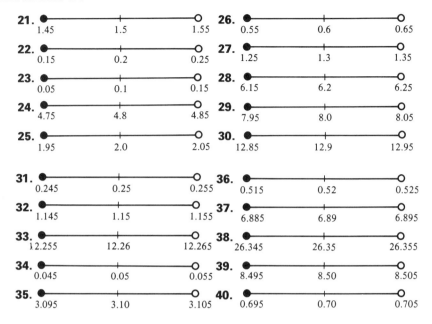

21. 1.45   1.5   1.55
22. 0.15   0.2   0.25
23. 0.05   0.1   0.15
24. 4.75   4.8   4.85
25. 1.95   2.0   2.05

26. 0.55   0.6   0.65
27. 1.25   1.3   1.35
28. 6.15   6.2   6.25
29. 7.95   8.0   8.05
30. 12.85   12.9   12.95

31. 0.245   0.25   0.255
32. 1.145   1.15   1.155
33. 12.255   12.26   12.265
34. 0.045   0.05   0.055
35. 3.095   3.10   3.105

36. 0.515   0.52   0.525
37. 6.885   6.89   6.895
38. 26.345   26.35   26.355
39. 8.495   8.50   8.505
40. 0.695   0.70   0.705

EXERCISE 1n
(p. 22)

1. $5.55 \leqslant w < 5.65$
2. $2450 \leqslant x < 2550$
3. $2.75 \leqslant x < 2.85$
4. $12.45 \leqslant x < 12.55$
5. $74\,500 \leqslant x \leqslant 75\,499$ (whole numbers only)
6. $1.245 \leqslant d < 1.255$
7. (a) $1.55\,\text{m} \leqslant \text{width} < 1.65\,\text{m}$
   (b) It may be too big
   (c) Not accurate enough for measuring the space for a new cupboard
8. 65 people
9. £54.99
10. $252.5 \leqslant \text{length} < 257.5$
11. 97.5 m
12. $395\,\text{g} \leqslant \text{weight of pack} < 405\,\text{g}$
13. $2985\,\text{cm} \leqslant \text{length} < 2995\,\text{cm}$; 10 cm

EXERCISE 1p
(p. 24)

1. a) 30   b) 42
2. a) $\frac{4}{3}$ b) $\frac{y}{x}$
3. a) $\frac{3}{2}$ b) $\frac{4}{9}$
4. $2\frac{3}{10}$
5. a) 3.36   b) 0.2943   c) 109
6. a) 16   b) 1   c) $\frac{1}{16}$
7. a) 5^2 b) 5^{12}
8. a) 2.56×10^3 b) 2.56×10^{-4}
9. $1.45\,\text{mm} \leqslant \text{diameter} < 1.55\,\text{mm}$
10. $65 \leqslant \text{number of children} \leqslant 74$ (whole numbers)

EXERCISE 1q
(p. 24)

1. a) 24 b) 30
2. a) 5 b) $\frac{2}{3}$
3. a) $\frac{3}{4}$ b) $1\frac{17}{20}$
4. a) $3\frac{1}{12}$
5. a) 1.45 b) 2.625 c) 0.42
6. a) $\frac{1}{4}$ b) 1 c) 4
7. a) 5.7×10^5 b) 5.7×10^{-2}
8. $445 \leqslant$ number of tacks $\leqslant 454$ (whole numbers)
9. $0.745\,\text{m} \leqslant$ diameter $< 0.755\,\text{m}$
10. $495\,\text{g} \leqslant$ weight $< 505\,\text{g}$

CHAPTER 2   Equations, Inequalities and Formulae

The first part of this chapter revises directed numbers, collection of like terms, and solution of linear equations.

EXERCISE 2a
(p. 27)

Can be used as a quick reminder of directed numbers.

1. $>$	3. $<$	5. $<$
2. $<$	4. $>$	6. $<$

7. -2	9. 3	11. -4
8. -11	10. 1	12. 0

13. -8	16. 12	19. -2
14. -2	17. -8	20. 48
15. 4	18. 2	21. 35

EXERCISE 2b
(p. 28)

Simplification of algebraic expressions, including practice in the use of directed numbers.

1. Not possible 6. $p+q$
2. $2a$ 7. $4x-2y$
3. Not possible 8. $5u$
4. $7v$ 9. $3b-a$
5. $2x$ 10. $4c+2d$

EXERCISE 2c
(p. 29)

1. xy 5. $\dfrac{u}{v}$

2. a^2 6. $\dfrac{-a}{b}$

3. $6s^2$ 7. 1

4. $12x^2$ 8. $\dfrac{3b}{c}$

9. Not possible

10. Not possible

11. $-mn$

12. Not possible

13. $-2a$

14. $4p^3$

15. $\dfrac{2u}{w}$

16. Not possible

17. $6st$

18. $2p^2$

19. $-4q$

20. $r+4s$

21. $\dfrac{4p}{q}$

22. $6st$

23. $-2b^2$

24. $\dfrac{x}{y}$

25. $3b-2a$

26. a^2-a

27. $3a-3b$

28. $6a-4c-2b$

29. $2z-y$

30. $6x+4y+2z$

31. $p+3q-2r$

32. $x-y$

33. $5q-p$

34. $a^2+ab-2a+2b$

35. x^2+y^2-2xy

36. $2b-6c$

37. $2p-2q$

38. w^2+x^2

39. $8n-2m$

40. $2b-8c$

EXERCISE 2d
(p. 31)

Can be used for discussion and as a reminder about the meaning of "equation" before beginning the work on inequalities.

1. $p = -\frac{2}{3}$

2. $s = \frac{1}{2}$

3. $x = 3\frac{1}{2}$

4. $a = \frac{1}{5}$

5. $x = 1$

6. $y = 1$

7. $x = 2$

8. $a = 4$

9. $x = \frac{1}{2}$

10. $x = 2$

11. $x = -\frac{1}{2}$

12. $x = -5$

13. $x = -\frac{1}{7}$

14. $y = 3\frac{1}{3}$

15. $x = 2\frac{4}{7}$

16. $x = 3\frac{2}{3}$

17. $a = -11$

18. $p = 0$

19. $w = 2$

20. $x = 5$

21. $x = 6\frac{1}{2}$

22. $x = -\frac{1}{6}$

23. $x = 2\frac{1}{2}$

24. $x = 1\frac{3}{4}$

25. $x = \frac{3}{14}$

26. $b = 19$

27. $x = \frac{5}{6}$

28. $x = -1$

29. $x = 2$

30. $x = \frac{1}{2}$

EXERCISE 2e
(p. 32)

Work in Exercise 1m should be discussed before this section. Numbers 10–15 can be used for discussion.

1. ○——— 7

2. ———○ 4

3. ○——— -2

4. ○——— 0

5. ———○ -2

6. ○——— $\frac{1}{2}$

7. ———○ 5

8. ———○ 0

9. ———○ 1.5

10. a) $2, 3, 4, 6, 7$
   b) $2, 5, 7, 8, 9$ c) $2, 3, 7, 9$
   d) $2, 3, 4, 6, 7$
   e) $2, 3, 4, 7, 9$

12. a) $5 > 3$; Yes
   b) $1 > -1$; Yes
   c) $-2 > -4$; Yes
   d) $7 > 5$; Yes

13. a) $0 > -1$; Yes b) $-4 > -5$; Yes
c) $-7 > -8$; Yes d) $2 > 1$; Yes
14. a) $1 < 6$; Yes b) $-3 < 2$; Yes
c) $-6 < -1$; Yes d) $3 < 8$; Yes

EXERCISE 2f Numbers 28–32 can be used for discussion.
(p. 33)

1. $x < 12$ ———○ 12   **6.** $x < 3$ ———○ 3

2. $x < 2$ ———○ 2   **7.** $x < -3$ ———○ -3

3. $x > 5$ ○——— 5   **8.** $x < -7$ ———○ -7

4. $x > 2$ ○——— 2   **9.** $x < -5$ ———○ -5

5. $x < -2$ ———○ -2

10. $x < -2$ ———○ -2 **15.** $x < -3$ ———○ -3

11. $x > -1$ ○——— -1 **16.** $x < 1$ ———○ 1

12. $x < 3$ ———○ 3   **17.** $x > -2$ ○——— -2

13. $x > 0$ ○——— 0   **18.** $x < -5$ ———○ -5

14. $x > -3$ ○——— -3

19. $x < 5$ ———○ 5   **24.** $x > -5$ ○——— -5

20. $x < 1$ ———○ 1   **25.** $x > -3$ ○——— -3

21. $x < -1$ ———○ -1 **26.** $x < 13$ ———○ 13

22. $x > 0$ ○——— 0   **27.** $x > 12$ ○——— 12

23. $x > 7$ ○——— 7

28. a) $24 < 72$ b) $3 < 9$ c) $6 < 18$
d) $2 < 6$ e) $-24 < -72$ f) $-4 < -12$
a) Yes   b) Yes   c) Yes   d) Yes   e) No   f) No

29. a) $72 > -24$ b) $9 > -3$ c) $18 > -6$
d) $6 > -2$ e) $-72 > 24$ f) $-12 > 4$
a) Yes   b) Yes   c) Yes   d) Yes   e) No   f) No

30. a) $-36 < -12$ b) $-4\frac{1}{2} < -1\frac{1}{2}$ c) $-9 < -3$
d) $-3 < -1$ e) $36 < 12$ f) $6 < 2$
a) Yes   b) Yes   c) Yes   d) Yes   e) No   f) No

32. Only when you are multiplying by a positive number.

EXERCISE 2g
(p. 35)

1. $x < 3$
2. $x > 1$
3. $x > 2$
4. $x < 1$

5. $x < \frac{1}{2}$
6. $x > 1\frac{1}{3}$
7. $x < 2\frac{1}{4}$
8. $x > 1\frac{1}{2}$

9. $x \leqslant 1$
10. $x \leqslant 4$
11. $x \geqslant -2$

12. $x \geqslant 1$
13. $x < -1$
14. $x \leqslant 2$

15. $x > 1$
16. $x \geqslant 1\frac{1}{3}$
17. $x \geqslant 0$

18. $x \leqslant 1$
19. $x < 1$
20. $x < -3$

21. a) $x > 3$ b) $2 \leqslant x \leqslant 3$
    c) No values of x
22. a) $0 \leqslant x \leqslant 1$ b) $x \leqslant 0$
    c) No values of x
23. a) $-2 < x \leqslant 4$ b) No values of x
    c) $x < -2$
24. a) $-3 < x < -1$ b) $x < -3$
    c) No values of x

25. $x < 12$; $x > -1$; $-1 < x < 12$
26. $x \leqslant -1$; $x \geqslant 3$; No values of x
27. $x \leqslant 7$; $x \geqslant -2$; $-2 \leqslant x \leqslant 7$
28. $x > 1$; $x < 2$; $1 < x < 2$

29. $x > 2$; $x < 3$; $2 < x < 3$
30. $x < 2$; $x > -1$; $-1 < x < 2$
31. $x \geqslant -1$; $x < 2$; $-1 \leqslant x < 2$

32. $x > \frac{1}{2}$; $x \leqslant 3$; $\frac{1}{2} < x \leqslant 3$

33. $2 < x < 5$
34. $-3 \leqslant x \leqslant 2$
35. $x < -2$
36. $0 < x < 2$
37. $x \geqslant 1$

38. $-4 < x < 2$
39. $x < -3$
40. $x < -1$
41. $1\frac{4}{5} < x < 3$
42. $\frac{1}{2} < x < 1$

EXERCISE 2h (p. 38) These problems are slightly harder than those in Book 2A. A general discussion on units is advisable and Numbers 11–20 can be used for this purpose, although the most able pupils can work through these on their own.

1. $a = b + c$
2. $m = 2(n + p)$
3. $z = xy$
4. $a = 2bc$
5. $v = n^2$
6. $d = e - f$
7. $x = \frac{y}{2}$

8. $a = \frac{b}{2c}$
9. $k = 2u + 3v$
10. $x = 2y - z$
11. $n = p + p^2$
12. $v = u + at$
13. $R = Np$
14. $y = nx$

15. $X = xy$
16. $N = y + z$
17. $P = \frac{x + y}{50}$
18. $b = \frac{ac}{1000}$
19. $n = 1 + 2m$
20. $R = \frac{x}{10} + \frac{y}{5}$

EXERCISE 2i (p. 40) Gives more practice in the use of directed numbers.

1. $p = 8$
2. $v = 2$
3. $z = \frac{3}{4}$
4. $a = 2$
5. $x = 25$
6. $C = 30$

7. $x = 24$
8. $p = 6$
9. $S = 10$
10. $v = -5$
11. $p = 4$
12. $a = 9$

13. $r = 2\frac{2}{3}$
14. $n = \frac{1}{2}$
15. $a = 2$
16. $V = 32$
17. $p = 21$
18. $a = 6$

EXERCISE 2j (p. 41) Numbers 1–20 require one operation. Numbers 21–36 require two operations. Some of these involve division of, say, $x + y$ by another letter or number. It is a good idea to encourage the use of brackets in this situation, e.g. $2a = x + y$, $2a = (x + y)$, $a = \frac{(x + y)}{2}$.

1. $s = p - r$
2. $y = x - 3$
3. $b = a + c$
4. $Y = X + Z$
5. $s = r - 2t$

6. $m = k - l$
7. $v = u + 5$
8. $y = z - x$
9. $P = N + Q$
10. $u = v - 10t$

11. $y = \frac{x}{2}$
12. $t = 2v$
13. $b = \frac{a}{c}$
14. $u = 3t$
15. $m = kl$

16. $b = \frac{a}{3}$
17. $N = 10X$
18. $u = \frac{v}{t}$
19. $w = 100z$
20. $p = qn$

21. $s = \dfrac{P-r}{2}$ **25.** $w = \dfrac{x+y}{2}$

22. $t = \dfrac{u-v}{3}$ **26.** $t = \dfrac{l-k}{4}$

23. $c = \dfrac{b-a}{4}$ **27.** $y = \dfrac{x-w}{6}$

24. $v = \dfrac{V-3u}{2}$ **28.** $s = \dfrac{It-N}{2}$

29. $y = \dfrac{4x}{3}$ **33.** $R = \dfrac{IV}{2}$

30. $t = \dfrac{u-v}{5}$ **34.** $r = \dfrac{p+w}{2}$

31. $I = 10(A-P)$ **35.** $c = 2(a-b)$

32. $y = 3(x-z)$ **36.** $r = 5(q-p)$

37. $u = v-at;\ u = 140$ **39.** $C = NP;\ C = 40$

38. $B = A - \dfrac{C}{100};\ B = 17.5$ **40.** $x = 2(z+3t);\ x = -10$

41. a) $a = b+2c$ b) $a = 4$ c) $b = a-2c$

42. a) $x = 2yz$ b) $x = 12$ c) $y = \dfrac{x}{2z}$

43. a) $d = e^2+2f$ b) $f = \dfrac{d-e^2}{2}$ c) $f = \frac{1}{2}$

44. a) $R = \dfrac{3xn}{25}$ b) $R = 4.8$

EXERCISE 2k **1.** a) Length   c) Area   e) Length
(p. 44)   b) Volume   d) Volume   f) Area
2. a) Length   c) Volume   e) Area
    b) Volume   d) Length   f) Area
3. a) cm   c) cm^2 e) cm
    b) cm^2 d) cm^3 f) cm^3
4. a) Area   d) Volume   g) Length
    b) Area   e) Volume   h) Area
    c) Length   f) Length   i) Area
5. (c) and (e) are wrong
6. $2r$ represents a length because it contains only one letter representing a length unit
7. 2

EXERCISE 2l **1.** a) -4 b) -1 c) -2
(p. 45)   **2.** a) $4x$ b) $6b$ c) $-3x^3$
3. a) $a+b$ b) $a+5b$
4. a) $x = 1\frac{1}{4}$ b) $x = 4\frac{2}{3}$
5. a) $x > 2$ b) $x \leqslant 6$ c) $-2 < x < 1\frac{1}{2}$

6. a) $r = \dfrac{v-u}{4}$ b) $r = \dfrac{ps}{5}$

7. a) $P = 37\frac{1}{2}$ b) 40

EXERCISE 2m	**1.** a) 13	b) 2	c) 4
(p. 46)	**2.** a) $10a - 3b$	b) $4x + x^2$	c) $12ab$
	3. a) $3y - 2x$	b) $2y - 6x$	
	4. a) $a = -1$	b) $x = \frac{7}{8}$	
	5. a) $x > 1$	b) $x > -1$	c) $-1 < x < 1$
	6. a) $d = \dfrac{C}{\pi}$	b) $d = \dfrac{a+s}{7}$	
	7. a) $u = 56$	b) $u = -86$	

CHAPTER 3   Sequences

EXERCISE 3a
(p. 47)   There are other possible ways of describing how to continue a sequence.

1. 25, 36, ... Square the next natural number

2. 15, 18, ... Add 3 to the previous term, or multiply the next natural number by 3

3. 35, 42, ... Add 7 to the previous term, or multiply the next natural number by 7

4. 10, 14, ... Add 4 to the previous term

5. $-1, -5, \ldots$ Take 4 from previous term

6. $\frac{1}{8}, \frac{1}{16}, \ldots$ Divide previous term by 2

7. 30, 42, ... Add to the previous term a number that increases by 2 each time

8. 720, 5040, ... Multiply the previous term by a number that increases by 1 each time

9. 15, ... 33, ...

10. 12, ...

11. 10, 12, 14, ...

12. $1, \frac{1}{2}, \frac{1}{4}, \ldots$

13. 8, 14, 22, ...

14. 18, 54, 162, ...

15. 6, 10, 16, ...

16. 0.01, 0.001, 0.0001, ...

17. $-1, -3, -5, \ldots$

18. $8, -16, 32, \ldots$

There are other possible answers to Numbers 19–22.

19. Multiply previous term by 3; add a number 4 greater than was added to previous term.

20. Add a number 2 greater than was added to previous term; double previous term and add 1.

21. Square the next natural number; add a number 2 greater than was added to previous term.

22. Multiply previous term by 2; add a number 3 greater than was added to previous term.

23. $\frac{1}{5}, \frac{1}{6}, \dots$

24. 13, 17, ...

25. 54, 6, ...

26. 45, 9, ...

27. 81, 5, ...

28. 16, 5, ...

29. a) (5, 26), ...   b) (10, 101), ...

30. 15, 21, 28, 36, ...

31. 1, 4, 9, 16, 25, ...

32. 1, 5, 14, 30, 55, ...

33. a) 13, 21, 34, ...   b) 2, 5, 7, 12, 19, 31, ...

34. 3, 12, 48, 192, 768, 3072, ...

EXERCISE 3b
(p. 50)

1. 3, 5, 7, 9, ...   15

2. 1, 3, 5, 7, ...   13

3. 2, 4, 8, 16, ...   128

4. 1, 4, 9, 16, ...   49

5. 0, 3, 8, 15, ...   48

6. 5, 6, 7, 8, ...   11

7. 5, 7, 9, 11, ...   17

8. $1, \frac{1}{2}, \frac{1}{3}, \frac{1}{4}, \dots$ $\frac{1}{7}$

EXERCISE 3c
(p. 51)

1. $3n$ **3.** $n+1$ **5.** $4n$

2. $-n$ **4.** $n-1$ **6.** 2^n

7. $2n+5$

8. $3n-3$ or $3(n-1)$

9. $\dfrac{1}{(n+2)}$

10. $n(n+2)$

11. n^3

12. $4-n$

13. $2n+4$, $8/2^n$, n^2-n+2, $2 \times 3^{n-1}$

14. a) 2 m   b) 20 m   c) $n(n+1)$ metres

CHAPTER 4 Matrices

EXERCISE 4a
(p. 54)

1. 2×2
2. 2×3
3. 2×1

4. 1×1
5. 1×3
6. 3×2

7. a) 6   b) 8   c) 2   d) 7

8. 3 1 7; $\begin{matrix} 4 \\ 7 \\ 2 \end{matrix}$ a) 7   b) 6   c) 4

9. $\begin{pmatrix} 0 & 0 & 0 \\ 1 & 1 & 1 \\ 2 & 2 & 2 \end{pmatrix}$

10. $\begin{pmatrix} 3 & 1 \\ 3 & 1 \\ 3 & 1 \end{pmatrix}$

EXERCISE 4b
(p. 56)

1. $\begin{pmatrix} 12 \\ 15 \end{pmatrix}$

2. $\begin{pmatrix} 15 & 4 \\ 7 & 1 \end{pmatrix}$

3. Not possible

4. (9, 5)

5. $\begin{pmatrix} 11 & 2 & 2 \\ 6 & 7 & 7 \end{pmatrix}$

6. $\begin{pmatrix} 11 & 11 \\ 11 & 5 \end{pmatrix}$

7. (5 3 5)

8. Not possible

9. $\begin{pmatrix} 6 & 8 \\ 7 & 7 \\ 7 & 7 \end{pmatrix}$

10. (10 8)

11. $\begin{pmatrix} 1 & 8 \\ -4 & 7 \end{pmatrix}$

12. $\begin{pmatrix} -2 \\ 2 \end{pmatrix}$

13. $\begin{pmatrix} -2 & 7 \\ -5 & 3 \end{pmatrix}$

14. (4 6)

15. $\begin{pmatrix} -3 \\ -3 \\ 6 \end{pmatrix}$

16. Not possible

17. $\begin{pmatrix} 2 & 10 \\ 5 & -3 \end{pmatrix}$

18. $\begin{pmatrix} 5 & -5 \\ 3 & 0 \end{pmatrix}$

19. $\begin{pmatrix} 0 & 8 \\ 8 & -2 \end{pmatrix}$

20. Not possible

21. Not possible
22. (1 6 −3)

23. $\begin{pmatrix} 2 & 3 & 4 \\ 5 & 0 & -12 \end{pmatrix}$

EXERCISE 4c
(p. 58)

1. $\begin{pmatrix} 3 \\ 6 \\ 12 \end{pmatrix}$

2. $\begin{pmatrix} 2 & 8 & 0 \\ 4 & -2 & 6 \end{pmatrix}$

3. $\begin{pmatrix} 1 & 2 \\ \frac{1}{2} & 3 \\ 1\frac{1}{2} & 4 \end{pmatrix}$

5. $\begin{pmatrix} -6 & -30 \\ 6 & 12 \end{pmatrix}$

4. $\begin{pmatrix} 6 & 24 \\ 18 & -12 \end{pmatrix}$

6. $\begin{pmatrix} 4 & 0 \\ \frac{2}{3} & 1\frac{1}{3} \\ 2 & 3\frac{1}{3} \end{pmatrix}$

7. $\begin{pmatrix} 2 & -2 \\ 1 & 3 \end{pmatrix}$

10. $\begin{pmatrix} 2 & 4 & 2 \\ -3 & -3 & -1 \end{pmatrix}$

8. Not possible

11. Not possible

9. $\begin{pmatrix} -3 \\ 3 \\ 0 \end{pmatrix}$

12. $\begin{pmatrix} -3 & -1 & 2 \\ 9 & 5 & 4 \\ 1 & 11 & 5 \end{pmatrix}$

EXERCISE 4d
(p. 59)

1. $\begin{pmatrix} -1 & 8 \\ 6 & 1 \end{pmatrix}$

7. $\begin{pmatrix} 2 & 8 \\ 6 & 4 \end{pmatrix}$

2. $\begin{pmatrix} 3 & 0 \\ 0 & 3 \end{pmatrix}$

8. $\begin{pmatrix} -1 & 2 \\ 1\frac{1}{2} & -\frac{1}{2} \end{pmatrix}$

3. Not possible

9. $\begin{pmatrix} 8 \\ 9 \\ 3 \end{pmatrix}$

4. $\begin{pmatrix} 7 & -1 \\ 5 & -1 \end{pmatrix}$

10. $\begin{pmatrix} 24 & 8 & -4 \\ 16 & 12 & 16 \end{pmatrix}$

5. $\begin{pmatrix} 1\frac{1}{3} \\ 1\frac{2}{3} \\ -\frac{1}{3} \end{pmatrix}$

11. Not possible

6. $\begin{pmatrix} -3 \\ -3 \\ -3 \end{pmatrix}$

12. $\begin{pmatrix} 8 & -2 & -2 \\ 1 & 4 & 4 \end{pmatrix}$

EXERCISE 4e
(p. 61)
A vector can be represented by a column matrix. Capital letters are used to denote matrices, including 2×1 column matrices, e.g. $\mathbf{A} = \begin{pmatrix} 1 \\ 4 \end{pmatrix}$, $\mathbf{B} = \begin{pmatrix} 5 & 2 \\ -4 & 3 \end{pmatrix}$, but a lower case letter is used when a column matrix represents a vector, e.g. $\mathbf{a} = \begin{pmatrix} 3 \\ -2 \end{pmatrix}$.

1. $\mathbf{B}$ 2×1, $\mathbf{C}$ 2×2, $\mathbf{D}$ 2×2, $\mathbf{E}$ 1×3, $\mathbf{F}$ 1×2, $\mathbf{G}$ 2×3

2. $\begin{pmatrix} 9 & 4 & 4 \\ 7 & 1 & 7 \end{pmatrix}$

6. Not possible

10. $\begin{pmatrix} 24 \\ 6 \end{pmatrix}$

3. Not possible

7. $(1\frac{1}{2}\ \ 1)$

11. $\begin{pmatrix} 4\frac{1}{2} & 1\frac{1}{2} \\ \frac{3}{4} & 3 \end{pmatrix}$

4. $\begin{pmatrix} 4 & -1 \\ 0 & 6 \end{pmatrix}$

8. Not possible

12. Not possible

5. $\begin{pmatrix} 12 & 9 & 3 \\ 3 & 6 & 9 \end{pmatrix}$

9. $\begin{pmatrix} 1 & -2 & 2 \\ 5 & -3 & 1 \end{pmatrix}$

13. Not possible

EXERCISE 4f
(p. 62) Here are two methods for remembering the order of matrix multiplication: (1) Calling the process "row–column" multiplication helps emphasize that rows are taken from the first matrix and columns from the second. (2) The picture of a person running along a diving board and then diving downwards gives the idea of "row first and then column".

1. $\begin{pmatrix}29\\27\end{pmatrix}$ 4. $\begin{pmatrix}9\\2\end{pmatrix}$ 7. $\begin{pmatrix}26\\10\end{pmatrix}$ 9. $\begin{pmatrix}56\\49\end{pmatrix}$

2. $\begin{pmatrix}14\\11\end{pmatrix}$ 5. $\begin{pmatrix}9\\5\end{pmatrix}$ 8. $\begin{pmatrix}58\\19\end{pmatrix}$ 10. $\begin{pmatrix}26\\10\end{pmatrix}$

3. $\begin{pmatrix}5\\7\end{pmatrix}$ 6. $\begin{pmatrix}18\\14\end{pmatrix}$

EXERCISE 4g
(p. 64)

1. $\begin{pmatrix}7\\10\end{pmatrix}$ 5. $\begin{pmatrix}19\\22\end{pmatrix}$

2. $\begin{pmatrix}14\\22\end{pmatrix}$ 6. $\begin{pmatrix}16\\12\end{pmatrix}$

3. $\begin{pmatrix}37\\2\end{pmatrix}$ 7. $\begin{pmatrix}12\\3\end{pmatrix}$

4. $\begin{pmatrix}23&16\end{pmatrix}$ 8. $\begin{pmatrix}17&19\\5\end{pmatrix}$

9. $\begin{pmatrix}22&52\\10&22\end{pmatrix}$ 12. $\begin{pmatrix}8&18\\18&36\end{pmatrix}$

10. $\begin{pmatrix}44&32\\8&7\end{pmatrix}$ 13. $\begin{pmatrix}44&40\\18&31\end{pmatrix}$

11. $\begin{pmatrix}16&14\\11&14\end{pmatrix}$ 14. $\begin{pmatrix}21&7\\17&9\end{pmatrix}$

15. $\begin{pmatrix}0&14\\10&8\end{pmatrix}$ 18. $\begin{pmatrix}-24&-17\\-10&-9\end{pmatrix}$

16. $\begin{pmatrix}15&20\\5&0\end{pmatrix}$ 19. $\begin{pmatrix}21&11\\9&2\end{pmatrix}$

17. $\begin{pmatrix}3&-4\\13&6\end{pmatrix}$ 20. $\begin{pmatrix}-16&1\\-6&-1\end{pmatrix}$

EXERCISE 4h
(p. 66)

1. $\begin{pmatrix}20&13\\8&5\end{pmatrix}$ 4. $\begin{pmatrix}44&29\\6&4\end{pmatrix}$ 7. $\begin{pmatrix}15&17\\31&35\end{pmatrix}$ 10. $\begin{pmatrix}4&2\\8&6\end{pmatrix}$

2. $\begin{pmatrix}10&7\\22&15\end{pmatrix}$ 5. $\begin{pmatrix}8&6\\4&2\end{pmatrix}$ 8. $\begin{pmatrix}46&31\\6&4\end{pmatrix}$ 11. $\begin{pmatrix}14&16\\2&2\end{pmatrix}$

3. $\begin{pmatrix}31&35\\15&17\end{pmatrix}$ 6. $\begin{pmatrix}8&6\\4&2\end{pmatrix}$ 9. $\begin{pmatrix}4&2\\8&6\end{pmatrix}$ 12. $\begin{pmatrix}14&16\\2&2\end{pmatrix}$

13. One of the two matrices was **D**

EXERCISE 4i
(p. 68)

1. $\begin{pmatrix} 7 \\ 10 \end{pmatrix}$

2. $\begin{pmatrix} 13 \\ 32 \end{pmatrix}$

5. $\begin{pmatrix} 32 & 26 & 16 \\ 20 & 19 & 11 \end{pmatrix}$

6. $\begin{pmatrix} 24 \\ 33 \\ 42 \end{pmatrix}$

7. $\begin{pmatrix} 21 & 39 & 8 \\ 17 & 26 & 7 \end{pmatrix}$

3. (10)

4. $\begin{pmatrix} 20 & 10 \\ 70 & 23 \end{pmatrix}$

8. $\begin{pmatrix} 10 & 11 \\ 36 & 30 \\ 31 & 28 \end{pmatrix}$

9. $(13 \ 31 \ 27)$

10. (15)

EXERCISE 4j
(p. 70)

1. $2 \times \boxed{2 \quad 2} \times 1 = 2 \times 1; \begin{pmatrix} 7 \\ 6 \end{pmatrix}$

2. $2 \times \boxed{3 \quad 3} \times 1 = 2 \times 1; \begin{pmatrix} 22 \\ 12 \end{pmatrix}$

3. $1 \times \boxed{2 \quad 2} \times 1 = 1 \times 1; \ (10)$

4. $2 \times \boxed{3 \quad 3} \times 2 = 2 \times 2; \begin{pmatrix} 20 & 10 \\ 70 & 23 \end{pmatrix}$

9. $\begin{pmatrix} 16 \\ 6 \end{pmatrix}$

10. Not possible

11. $\begin{pmatrix} 11 & 20 \\ 24 & 43 \end{pmatrix}$

12. Not possible

13. $\begin{pmatrix} 15 & 4 & 3 \\ 48 & 13 & 12 \end{pmatrix}$

5. $2 \times \boxed{2 \quad 2} \times 2 = 2 \times 2; \begin{pmatrix} 11 & 20 \\ 24 & 43 \end{pmatrix}$

6. $2 \times \boxed{1 \quad 1} \times 2 = 2 \times 2; \begin{pmatrix} 3 & 4 \\ 6 & 8 \end{pmatrix}$

7. $1 \times \boxed{2 \quad 2} \times 2 = 1 \times 2; \ (21 \ 36)$

8. $3 \times \boxed{1 \quad 1} \times 3 = 3 \times 3; \begin{pmatrix} 4 & 5 & 6 \\ 8 & 10 & 12 \\ 12 & 15 & 18 \end{pmatrix}$

14. Not possible

15. (30)

16. Not possible

17. $(3 \ 24)$

18. $\begin{pmatrix} 6 & 12 & 15 \\ 8 & 16 & 20 \\ 2 & 4 & 5 \end{pmatrix}$

EXERCISE 4k
(p. 71)

1. $\begin{pmatrix} 6 \\ 5 \end{pmatrix}$

2. $\begin{pmatrix} 10 \\ -19 \end{pmatrix}$

3. $(-2 \ -6)$

4. $\begin{pmatrix} 1 \\ 1 \\ -22 \end{pmatrix}$

5. $\begin{pmatrix} 8 & -26 \\ -16 & -17 \end{pmatrix}$

6. $(-38 \ 12)$

7. (-26)

8. $\begin{pmatrix} -24 & -4 & 12 \\ 6 & 1 & -3 \\ 6 & 1 & -3 \end{pmatrix}$

9. $\begin{pmatrix} 7 & 18 & -1 \\ -7 & -18 & 1 \end{pmatrix}$

10. $\begin{pmatrix} 12 & 18 \\ 8 & 12 \\ -6 & -9 \end{pmatrix}$

EXERCISE 4l
(p. 72)

1. $\begin{pmatrix} 13 & -8 \\ 7 & -2 \end{pmatrix}$

2. $\begin{pmatrix} 2 & -1 \\ 12 & 9 \end{pmatrix}$

3. $\begin{pmatrix} 10 \\ 5 \end{pmatrix}$

4. Not possible

5. $\begin{pmatrix} 3 & 4 \\ 6 & 8 \end{pmatrix}$

6. Not possible

7. Not possible

8. Not possible

9. Not possible

10. (11)

11. (14 6)

12. Not possible

13. Not possible

14. (9 12)

15. Not possible

16. $\mathbf{AA} = \begin{pmatrix} 19 & 18 \\ 6 & 7 \end{pmatrix}$ $\quad$ $\mathbf{AC} = \begin{pmatrix} 21 & 8 \\ 4 & 2 \end{pmatrix}$ $\quad$ $\mathbf{BB} = \begin{pmatrix} -5 & -2 \\ 3 & -6 \end{pmatrix}$

$\mathbf{BC} = \begin{pmatrix} 8 & 2 \\ 18 & 6 \end{pmatrix}$ $\quad$ $\mathbf{BD} = \begin{pmatrix} -3 \\ 3 \end{pmatrix}$ $\quad$ $\mathbf{CA} = \begin{pmatrix} 26 & 22 \\ -4 & -3 \end{pmatrix}$

$\mathbf{CB} = \begin{pmatrix} 12 & -12 \\ -1 & 2 \end{pmatrix}$ $\quad$ $\mathbf{CC} = \begin{pmatrix} 34 & 12 \\ -6 & -2 \end{pmatrix}$ $\quad$ $\mathbf{CD} = \begin{pmatrix} 10 \\ -1 \end{pmatrix}$

$\mathbf{DH} = \begin{pmatrix} 3 \\ 6 \end{pmatrix}$ $\quad$ $\mathbf{EA} = (16 \ 17)$ $\quad$ $\mathbf{EB} = (15 \ -6)$

$\mathbf{FE} = \begin{pmatrix} 18 & 24 \\ 3 & 4 \\ -12 & -16 \end{pmatrix}$ $\quad$ $\mathbf{FH} = \begin{pmatrix} 18 \\ 3 \\ -12 \end{pmatrix}$ $\quad$ $\mathbf{GF} = \begin{pmatrix} -4 \\ 15 \\ 5 \end{pmatrix}$

$\mathbf{GG} = \begin{pmatrix} 18 & -2 & 17 \\ -13 & 35 & 11 \\ 23 & 4 & 27 \end{pmatrix}$ $\quad$ $\mathbf{HH} = (9)$

EXERCISE 4m
(p. 73)

1. $\begin{pmatrix} 8 & 2 \\ -21 & -8 \end{pmatrix}$

2. $\begin{pmatrix} 7 & 4 \\ -3 & 3 \end{pmatrix}$

3. $\begin{pmatrix} -5 & 0 \\ -5 & 3 \end{pmatrix}$

4. $\begin{pmatrix} 5 & 0 \\ 5 & -3 \end{pmatrix}$

5. Not possible

6. Not possible

7. $(-2 \ -3)$

8. $\begin{pmatrix} -2 & 1 \\ 8 & 12 \end{pmatrix}$

9. $\begin{pmatrix} 5 & 3 & 3 \\ 11 & 5 & 9 \\ 2 & 2 & 0 \end{pmatrix}$

10. Not possible

11. Not possible

12. (4 2)

EXERCISE 4n
(p. 74)

1. $\begin{pmatrix} 12 & 10 \\ -2 & 13 \end{pmatrix}$

2. $\begin{pmatrix} 78 & -10 \\ 31 & -13 \end{pmatrix}$

3. $\begin{pmatrix} 13 & -6 \\ 18 & 1 \end{pmatrix}$

4. $\begin{pmatrix} 68 & 16 \\ 61 & 4 \end{pmatrix}$

5. $\begin{pmatrix} 48 & 40 \\ 38 & 17 \end{pmatrix}$

6. $\begin{pmatrix} 34 & -25 \\ 75 & -16 \end{pmatrix}$

7. $\begin{pmatrix} 78 & 8 \\ 31 & 28 \end{pmatrix}$

8. $\begin{pmatrix} 50 & 27 \\ 32 & 56 \end{pmatrix}$

9. $\begin{pmatrix} 55 & -11 \\ 66 & -22 \end{pmatrix}$

10. $\begin{pmatrix} -16 & 56 \\ -56 & 20 \end{pmatrix}$

11. $\begin{pmatrix} -64 & 0 \\ 0 & -64 \end{pmatrix}$

12. $\begin{pmatrix} 68 & -12 \\ 61 & -7 \end{pmatrix}$

EXERCISE 4p
(p. 74)

1. 2×2 and 2×1
2. Yes
3. **A**, **C** are compatible but not **C**, **A**
4. $\begin{pmatrix} 23 & -11 \\ 19 & -13 \end{pmatrix}$
5. $\mathbf{A}^2 = \begin{pmatrix} 27 & 18 \\ 9 & 18 \end{pmatrix}.$ It is not possible to find $\mathbf{C}^2$
6. Not possible
7. $\begin{pmatrix} 9 & -3 \\ 12 & -9 \end{pmatrix}$ **8.** $\begin{pmatrix} 13 & 3 \\ 6 & 5 \end{pmatrix}$ **9.** 4   **10.** BC

EXERCISE 4q
(p. 75)

1. $\begin{pmatrix} 4 & 2 & -2 \\ 8 & 6 & 2 \end{pmatrix}$
2. Not possible
3. Not possible
4. 2×3 and 2×2
5. No
6. 3
7. 1
8. QP
9. $\begin{pmatrix} 17 \\ 13 \end{pmatrix}$
10. It is not possible to find $\mathbf{P}^2$. $\mathbf{Q}^2 = \begin{pmatrix} 7 & 14 \\ -7 & 14 \end{pmatrix}$

CHAPTER 5   Percentages

For all but the best pupils, the early work in this chapter requires constant revision. The rest of this chapter concentrates on percentage increase and decrease in a variety of situations. It is the vocabulary and not the mathematics that often leads to difficulty here, so make sure that the pupils understand terms such as VAT, depreciation, percentage profit, etc.

EXERCISE 5a
(p. 76)

	Fraction	Percentage	Decimal
1.	$\frac{3}{5}$	60%	0.6
2.	$\frac{2}{5}$	40%	0.4
3.	$\frac{11}{20}$	55%	0.55
4.	$\frac{17}{20}$	85%	0.85

Fraction	Percentage	Decimal
5. $\frac{27}{50}$	54%	0.54
6. $\frac{6}{25}$	24%	0.24
7. $\frac{23}{25}$	92%	0.92
8. $\frac{21}{25}$	84%	0.84
9. $\frac{37}{40}$	$92\frac{1}{2}$%	0.925
10. $\frac{2}{3}$	$66\frac{2}{3}$%	$0.\dot{6}$

11. 24% **14.** 40% **17.** 5% **20.** 27%
12. 64% **15.** 25% **18.** 2.5% **21.** 40%
13. 20% **16.** 34% **19.** 2% **22.** 225%

23. 75 **26.** 0.54 km **29.** 2.5% **32.** 2.5%
24. 92 p **27.** 189 g **30.** 2% **33.** 2.4%
25. 0.61 cm **28.** 42 m² **31.** 1.5%

34. 60% **37.** 949 **40.** 381 **42.** 348
35. 30% **38.** 1007 **41.** 49.28 **43.** 31.59
36. 89.6% **39.** 627

44. 172 **46.** 294 **48.** 59.4 kg **50.** 102
45. 64.68 **47.** 5.74 **49.** £9675

EXERCISE 5b (p. 81) Numbers 23–30: Many teachers may prefer to use the idea of a multiplying factor as a slight variation of Method 2 in the worked example.

i.e. if the rate of VAT is 15%

$$\text{Purchase price} = \text{marked price} \times 1.15 \text{ or } \frac{115}{100}$$

The idea may be used in many problems on percentages.

1. 25% **3.** 25% **5.** 20% **7.** 15%
2. 30% **4.** 10% **6.** 20% **8.** 24%

9. £56 **12.** £18 **15.** £12 **18.** £24.30
10. £72 **13.** £27 **16.** £21.60 **19.** £21
11. £60.90 **14.** £80 **17.** £18

20. (b) by £8 **23.** £34.50 **26.** £43.70
21. (b) by 70 p **24.** £75.52 **27.** £690
22. the same **25.** £9.87 **28.** £9.20

22   *ST(P) Mathematics 3A*

EXERCISE 5c
(p. 83)

1. £1500	**4.** £3750	**7.** £3300	**10.** £7680
2. £2400	**5.** £1935	**8.** £2240	**11.** £1800
3. £1950	**6.** £2478	**9.** £4000	**12.** £2100

13. £2950	**16.** £28	**19.** £58
14. £2112	**17.** £92	**20.** £33.60
15. £4270	**18.** £25.60	**21.** £38.25

22. £16.15	**24.** £32.25
23. £14.30	**25.** a) £12.20 b) £14.80

EXERCISE 5d
(p. 86) More teaching effort is usually required with this topic than for most other percentage questions. Multiplying factors can also be used here.

1. £70	**6.** £32	**11.** £40	**16.** £50
2. £40	**7.** £800	**12.** £80	**17.** £160
3. £16	**8.** £900	**13.** £200	**18.** £17
4. £6	**9.** £800	**14.** £18	**19.** £160
5. £2.70	**10.** £20	**15.** £13.60	**20.** £2000

21. £120	**26.** £12
22. £125	**27.** £650
23. £260	**28.** £160
24. £184	**29.** 850 cm³
25. £92	**30.** 25 cm

EXERCISE 5e
(p. 88)

1. £77 520	**4.** 40%	**7.** 212.5 cm³	**10.** 44 275
2. £13.69	**5.** £1200	**8.** £172	**11.** a) £7.20 b) £6.60
3. 33⅓%	**6.** £37.50	**9.** 15 km/l	**12.** £280

EXERCISE 5f
(p. 90)

1. £60	**6.** £373.76
2. £731.35	**7.** 8.5%
3. £26.40	**8.** £500
4. £925	**9.** £250
5. £215.80	

EXERCISE 5g
(p. 91)

1. £42	**4.** £191.77	**7.** £252.68	**10.** £1093.50
2. £76.32	**5.** £143.99	**8.** £48 400	**11.** £12 800
3. £103.88	**6.** £206.72	**9.** £76	

CHAPTER 6   Straight Line Graphs

This chapter revises and slightly extends the work in Book 2A. The diagrams for Exercise 6a can be done on squared paper as can some of the graphs in Exercise 6b, but graph paper should be used fairly soon so that values can be read more accurately.

EXERCISE 6a
(p. 94)

1. $x = 4$ **2.** $y = 5$ **3.** $y = -3$ **4.** $x = -2$

5. 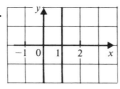   **6.**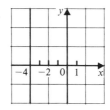

7. 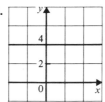   **8.**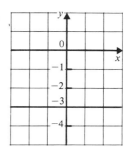

EXERCISE 6b
(p. 96)

The graphs drawn for Numbers 5–8 are used for Numbers 17–20 so Numbers 17–20 can be done at the same time as Numbers 5–8.

1.

x	-2	0	4
y	2	4	8

3.

x	-3	0	3
y	7	4	1

2.

x	-2	0	3
y	-3	1	7

4.

x	-1	0	3
y	5	2	-4

13. a) $1\frac{1}{2}$ b) 0.4   c) -1.6
14. a) 0   b) -0.8 c) -3.4
15. a) -2.6 b) -1.8 c) 1.2
16. a) 3.6   b) 0.6   c) 1.2
17. a) $-2\frac{1}{2}$ b) 4.4   c) 2.4
18. a) 4.8   b) 1.2   c) -11.2
19. a) -1.4 b) 1.4   c) 3.5
20. a) 8.6   b) 2.8   c) 3

EXERCISE 6c
(p. 99)

1. Yes, No   **4.** No, Yes
2. Yes, Yes   **5.** Yes, Yes
3. No, No   **6.** No, Yes

EXERCISE 6d Squared paper can be used for this exercise.
(p. 100)
     1. Lines are parallel; coefficient of x is 2 in each equation
     2. Lines are parallel; coefficient of x is -3 in each equation
     3. Lines are parallel; coefficient of x is $\frac{1}{2}$ in each equation
     4. Lines are parallel; coefficient of x is 1 in each equation
     5. Lines (a) and (c) are parallel
     6. Lines are parallel; coefficient of x is -1 in each equation

EXERCISE 6e Squared paper can be used for this exercise. Number 8 provides another
(p. 103) opportunity to emphasise that division by zero is not possible. In general, if a line
is parallel to the y-axis avoid talking about the value of its gradient.

     1. 4   **2.** -2 **3.** 1   **4.** $-\frac{3}{4}$ **5.** $-\frac{9}{5}$ **6.** $\frac{2}{3}$
     7. 0
     8. y-axis. You find yourself dividing by zero
     9. a) Parallel to the y-axis   b) Zero gradient
          c) Zero gradient   d) Parallel to the y-axis

EXERCISE 6f **1.** 2   **2.** 1   **3.** 2   **4.** -2
(p. 104 **5.** 4   **6.** a) 4   b) -3 c) 1   d) $\frac{1}{2}$

     7. a)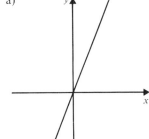   b)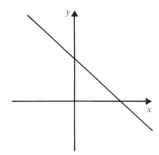

     8. a)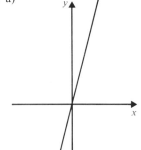   b)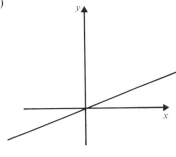

9. a) 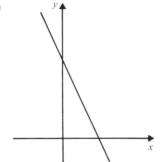 b)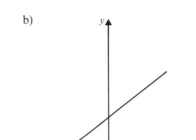

EXERCISE 6g	**1.** $2, 4$	**4.** $1, -6$	**7.** $5, 2$	**11.** $-3, 7$
(p. 106)	**2.** $5, 3$	**5.** $-2, 3$	**8.** $\frac{1}{2}, -1$	**12.** $\frac{1}{3}, 7$
	3. $3, -4$	**6.** $-4, 2$	**9.** $-\frac{1}{3}, 4$	**13.** $-0.4, 9$
			10. $3, -7$	**14.** $5, 4$

15. $2, 2\frac{1}{2}$ **19.** $y = 2x + 7$ **23.** $y = \frac{1}{2}x + 6$
16. $\frac{1}{3}, -2$ **20.** $y = 3x + 1$ **24.** $y = -2x + 1$
17. $\frac{2}{5}, 1$ **21.** $y = x + 3$ **25.** $y = x - 2$
18. $-\frac{3}{4}, 2$ **22.** $y = 2x - 5$ **26.** $y = -\frac{1}{2}x + 4$

EXERCISE 6h
(p. 108)

1. $y = 3x + 1$, $y = 5 + 3x$, $y = 3x - 4$
2. $y = 2 - x$, $y = 4 - x$, $2y = 3 - 2x$, $y = -x + 1$, $y = -x$
3. $3y = x$, $y = \frac{1}{3}x + 2$, $y = \frac{1}{3} + \frac{1}{3}x$, $y = \frac{1}{3}x - 4$
4. $y = \frac{1}{2}x + 2$ and $y = \frac{1}{2}x - 1$; $y = 2 - \frac{1}{2}x$ and $2y = 3 - x$
5. 2; $y = 2x + 3$
6. -3; $y = -3x + 1$
7. $y = 4x$
8. e.g. $y = 6 - x$, $y = -x$, $y = -2 - x$
9. a) $y = 4x + 4$ b) $y = -3x + 4$ c) $y = \frac{1}{2}x + 4$
10. a) $y = \frac{1}{3}x + 6$ b) $y = \frac{1}{3}x$ c) $y = \frac{1}{3}x - 3$
11. a) $y = 2x + 2$ b) $y = 2x + 10$ c) $y = 2x - 4$
12. $y = 3 + 2x$ and $y = 2x - 3$
13. $-3, 4$; $4, -3$; $y = -3x - 3$
14. a) $y = -4x$ b) $y = -4x - 7$

EXERCISE 6i	**1.** $-\frac{3}{5}$	**4.** -1	**7.** $\frac{1}{3}$
(p. 110)	**2.** $-\frac{1}{3}$	**5.** -2	**8.** 2
	3. $\frac{1}{4}$	**6.** $-\frac{1}{3}$	**9.** -1 in each case

EXERCISE 6j	**1.** $-\frac{3}{4}$	**3.** $\frac{1}{2}$	**5.** 2
(p. 111)	**2.** $-\frac{3}{5}$	**4.** -2	**6.** $\frac{3}{4}$

7. a) $(2,0), (0,4)$ b) $(12,0), (0,-9)$

8. a) $\dfrac{x}{6}+\dfrac{y}{5}=1$ b) $\dfrac{x}{4}-\dfrac{y}{3}=1$

9. $-\dfrac{1}{3}$

EXERCISE 6k
(p. 112)

1. $-\frac{3}{5}, 3$ **3.** $\frac{1}{4}, -2$ **5.** $3, 6$

2. $-\frac{1}{3}, 2$ **4.** $\frac{1}{3}, -2$ **6.** $-\frac{1}{3}, 2$

7. $-\frac{3}{4}, 3$ **10.** $-3, 6$ **13.** $4, 2$

8. $-\frac{3}{5}, 3$ **11.** $-\frac{4}{3}, 4$ **14.** $-1, 4$

9. $\frac{1}{2}, -2$ **12.** $\frac{4}{3}, -4$ **15.** $-2, 4$

16. $-\frac{2}{5}, 3$ **18.** $2, \frac{5}{2}$ **20.** $-1, -3$

17. $-\frac{1}{2}, 5$ **19.** $2, -4$ **21.** $-\frac{3}{4}, 3$

EXERCISE 6l
(p. 114)

1. $-\frac{4}{3}, 4; y = -\frac{4}{3}x+4$ **4.** $-\frac{4}{3}, 2; y = -\frac{4}{3}x+2$

2. $-2, 7; y = -2x+7$ **5.** $\frac{7}{2}, -4; y = \frac{7}{2}x-4$

3. $\frac{3}{5}, 1; y = \frac{3}{5}x+1$ **6.** $\frac{1}{3}, -1; y = \frac{1}{3}x-1$

7. $\frac{1}{6}, 1; y = \frac{1}{6}x+1$ **10.** $-1, -5; y = -x-5$

8. $\frac{4}{5}, -3; y = \frac{4}{5}x-3$ **11.** $2, 12; y = 2x+12$

9. $\frac{5}{3}, -4; y = \frac{5}{3}x-4$ **12.** $\frac{5}{6}, 6; y = \frac{5}{6}x+6$

13. $AB, 5y = 2x+20; AC, 5x+3y = 12$

14. $3, y = 3x-11$ **19.** $-1, y = -x+3$

15. $-3, y = -3x+7$ **20.** $-1, y = -x+1$

16. $\frac{5}{2}, y = \frac{5}{2}x-\frac{1}{2}$ **21.** $2, y = 2x-11$

17. $2, y = 2x+7$ **22.** $\frac{1}{5}, y = \frac{1}{5}x-\frac{6}{5}$

18. $5, y = 5x-21$ **23.** $-\frac{5}{2}, y = -\frac{5}{2}x+\frac{19}{2}$

24. $-\frac{5}{4}, \dfrac{x}{4}+\dfrac{y}{5}=1$ or $y = -\frac{5}{4}x+5$

25. $-\frac{2}{3}, \dfrac{x}{3}+\dfrac{y}{2}=1$ or $y = -\frac{2}{3}x+2$

26. $\frac{2}{3}, \dfrac{x}{3}-\dfrac{y}{2}=1$ or $y = \frac{2}{3}x-2$

27. $-3, \dfrac{x}{2}+\dfrac{y}{6}=1$ or $y = -3x+6$

28. $3, y = 3x-10$ **30.** $-\frac{7}{2}, y = -\frac{7}{2}x-6$

29. $-1, y = -x+4$ **31.** $-1, y = -x+3$

32. $\frac{5}{2}, -\dfrac{x}{2}+\dfrac{y}{5}=1$ or $y = \frac{5}{2}x+5$

33. $\frac{2}{11}$, $y = \frac{2}{11}x + \frac{21}{11}$ **35.** $-\frac{1}{4}$, $y = -\frac{1}{4}x + \frac{11}{4}$
34. 1, $y = x - 1$

EXERCISE 6m **1.** $y = 3x - 16$ **5.** Midpoint is $(5,3)$; $y = -2x + 13$
(p. 116) **2.** Square   **6.** $2y = -x + 4$
3. Rhombus   **7.** Square
4. $(\frac{1}{2}, 3)$

EXERCISE 6n **1.** 2   **4.** 12   **7.** Yes
(p. 117) **2.** $(0, 4)$ **5.** $y = 5x$ **8.** $\frac{3}{5}$
3. $(4, 0)$ **6.** $(12, 0)$

EXERCISE 6p **1.** -3 **4.** $(0, 4)$ **7.** $y = \frac{1}{2}x$
(p. 117) **2.** No   **5.** $(0, 6), (6, 0)$ **8.** $(2, 0), (0, 3)$
3. $y = -4x$ **6.** $-\frac{3}{2}$

CHAPTER 7 Simultaneous Equations

This chapter concentrates on solution by elimination. Matrix solution of simultaneous equations is in Chapter 8.

EXERCISE 7a **1.** $3, 2$ **4.** $1, 7$ **7.** $-2, 1$ **10.** $6, 0$
(p. 119) **2.** $2, 4$ **5.** $4, -3$ **8.** $5, 1$ **11.** $-1, -2$
3. $3, 5$ **6.** $2, 5$ **9.** $3, 1\frac{1}{2}$ **12.** $0, 9$

EXERCISE 7b When using addition to eliminate it is usually easier to eliminate the second letter,
(p. 120) but common-sense is needed!

1. $3, 1$ **6.** $9, 1$ **11.** $2, 3$ **16.** $\frac{1}{2}, 4$
2. $4, 2$ **7.** $4, -2$ **12.** $4, -1$ **17.** $4, -2$
3. $3, 4$ **8.** $1, 0$ **13.** $6, 2$ **18.** $-3, 1$
4. $3, -1$ **9.** $0, 6$ **14.** $5, 1\frac{1}{2}$ **19.** $2, \frac{1}{3}$
5. $3, \frac{1}{2}$ **10.** $2, 3$ **15.** $4, 3$ **20.** $3, -2$

21. $3, 2$ **24.** $1\frac{1}{2}, 2$ **27.** $6, 2$ **30.** $-1, -2$
22. $4, 5$ **25.** $-3, 2$ **28.** $4, 3$ **31.** $5, 4$
23. $3, 0$ **26.** $4, -2$ **29.** $-1, 4$ **32.** $2, -4$

EXERCISE 7c **1.** $3, 1$ **4.** $-12, 27$ **7.** $1, 2$ **10.** $0, 3$
(p. 123) **2.** $1, 2$ **5.** $0, 1$ **8.** $2, 1$ **11.** $1, -1$
3. $\frac{1}{3}, 1$ **6.** $4, 3$ **9.** $3, -1$ **12.** $3, \frac{1}{2}$

EXERCISE 7d
(p. 124)

1. $3, 2$	**5.** $0, 6$	**9.** $2, 2$	**13.** $2, \frac{2}{3}$
2. $1, 5$	**6.** $3, -1$	**10.** $3, -1$	**14.** $-1, 2$
3. $3, 1$	**7.** $1, 4$	**11.** $4, 2$	**15.** $3, -2$
4. $1\frac{1}{2}, 0$	**8.** $1, 1$	**12.** $-3, 0$	**16.** $2, -2$

17. $0, 4$	**20.** $3, 1$	**23.** $-3, 4$	**26.** $2, 5$
18. $-1, -2$	**21.** $2, -1$	**24.** $3, -3\frac{1}{2}$	**27.** $3, 2$
19. $1, 1$	**22.** $8, 4$	**25.** $3, 4$	**28.** $-1, -3$

EXERCISE 7e
(p. 125)

1. $1, 4$	**6.** $-1, -1$
2. $-1, 5$	**7.** $3\frac{1}{2}, 2\frac{1}{2}$
3. $3, -2$	**8.** $1, -2$
4. $6, 28$	**9.** $5, 0$
5. $2, 3$	**10.** $0, 4$

11. $3, 1$	**12.** $-4, -5$

EXERCISE 7f
(p. 126)
Can be omitted.

1. $2, 4$	**4.** $-2, 7$	**7.** $1, 10$	**10.** $-12, -4$
2. $5, 3$	**5.** $4, 6$	**8.** $2\frac{1}{3}, -\frac{2}{3}$	**11.** $2, 6$
3. $1, 1$	**6.** $1, 1$	**9.** $-1, 5$	**12.** $4\frac{1}{2}, 7\frac{1}{2}$

EXERCISE 7h
(p. 128)
Most children find these difficult. Only the most able should work from Number 7 onwards on their own.

1. $12, 8$	**4.** $10, 3$
2. $11, 5$	**5.** $10, 6$
3. $8, 2$	**6.** $11, 5$

7. $3, 7$	**11.** Harry 32, Adam 10, Sam 20
8. $54, 36$	**12.** $3, 5$
9. $60\,\text{p}, 45\,\text{p}$	**13.** $AB = 9\frac{1}{2}\,\text{cm}, BC = 6\,\text{cm}$
10. $25\,\text{p}, 10\,\text{p}$	**14.** $m = 2, c = 4, y = 2x + 4$

EXERCISE 7i
(p. 131)
The graphical solution of linear simultaneous equations is not a satisfactory method (it takes too long) but the idea is needed later for solving non-linear equations. The use of graph paper is essential for this exercise as most of the solutions are fractional (integer solutions can often be spotted when the tables are being made). A graphics calculator or a computer with graph-drawing software (with zoom facility) can be used to show how accurate and quick this method can be with appropriate tools.

1. $1\frac{1}{2}, 4\frac{1}{2}$	**6.** $1\frac{1}{2}, 3\frac{1}{2}$
2. $1\frac{1}{3}, 3\frac{2}{3}$	**7.** $2\frac{2}{5}, 1\frac{4}{5}$
3. $1\frac{1}{2}, 5\frac{1}{2}$	**8.** $-\frac{2}{5}, 1\frac{3}{5}$
4. $-\frac{1}{2}, 1\frac{1}{2}$	**9.** $2\frac{2}{5}, 1\frac{1}{5}$
5. $\frac{1}{2}, 2$	**10.** $\frac{1}{3}, 1\frac{2}{3}$

CHAPTER 8   Inverse and Square Matrices

Several topics in this chapter are not essential so selection may be necessary. However inverse matrices are needed for later work on transformations.

EXERCISE 8a **1.** Yes, 3×3 **3.** Yes, 2×2 **5.** Yes, 2×2
(p. 132)   **2.** No   **4.** No   **6.** Yes, 3×3

EXERCISE 8b **1.** $\begin{pmatrix} 4 & 7 \\ 7 & 11 \end{pmatrix}$ **7.** $\begin{pmatrix} 11 & 7 \\ 7 & 4 \end{pmatrix}$
(p. 133)

2. $(7 \ -6)$ **8.** Not possible

3. $\begin{pmatrix} 7 & 10 & 1 \\ 15 & 26 & 1 \end{pmatrix}$ **9.** $\begin{pmatrix} 4 & 24 & 4 \\ 3 & 18 & 3 \\ 2 & 12 & 2 \end{pmatrix}$

4. Not possible   **10.** (24)

5. Not possible   **11.** $\begin{pmatrix} 1 \\ -1 \end{pmatrix}$

6. $\begin{pmatrix} 26 & 13 \\ -4 & -2 \end{pmatrix}$ **12.** $(34 \ 6)$

EXERCISE 8c **1.** $\begin{pmatrix} 4 & 2 \\ 3 & 4 \end{pmatrix}$ **4.** $\begin{pmatrix} 0 & 0 \\ 0 & 0 \end{pmatrix}$
(p. 134)

2. $\begin{pmatrix} 4 \\ 5 \end{pmatrix}$ **5.** $(3 \ 2)$

3. $(0 \ 0)$ **6.** $\begin{pmatrix} 3 & 2 & -1 \\ 4 & 3 & 1 \end{pmatrix}$

EXERCISE 8d **1.** $\begin{pmatrix} 1 & 0 \\ 0 & 1 \end{pmatrix}$ **5.** $\begin{pmatrix} 3 & 0 \\ 0 & 3 \end{pmatrix}$
(p. 135)

2. $\begin{pmatrix} 5 & 0 \\ 0 & 5 \end{pmatrix}$ **6.** $\begin{pmatrix} 3 & 0 \\ 0 & 3 \end{pmatrix}$

3. $\begin{pmatrix} 5 & 0 \\ 0 & 5 \end{pmatrix}$ **7.** $\begin{pmatrix} -1 & 0 \\ 0 & -1 \end{pmatrix}$

4. $\begin{pmatrix} 2 & 0 \\ 0 & 2 \end{pmatrix}$ **8.** $\begin{pmatrix} 1 & 0 \\ 0 & 1 \end{pmatrix}$

10. $\begin{pmatrix} 6 & -2 \\ -8 & 3 \end{pmatrix}$ **13.** $\begin{pmatrix} 5 & 3 \\ -1 & 1 \end{pmatrix}$ **16.** $\begin{pmatrix} 8 & -4 \\ -9 & 5 \end{pmatrix}$

11. $\begin{pmatrix} 3 & -1 \\ -2 & 2 \end{pmatrix}$ **14.** $\begin{pmatrix} 4 & -7 \\ -3 & 5 \end{pmatrix}$ **17.** $\begin{pmatrix} 4 & -2 \\ -14 & 6 \end{pmatrix}$

12. $\begin{pmatrix} 3 & 1 \\ 20 & 6 \end{pmatrix}$ **15.** $\begin{pmatrix} 6 & -3 \\ -9 & 5 \end{pmatrix}$ **18.** $\begin{pmatrix} 1 & -2 \\ -2 & 1 \end{pmatrix}$

19. $\begin{pmatrix} -2 & 3 \\ -3 & 4 \end{pmatrix}$

EXERCISE 8e
(p. 137)

1. $\begin{pmatrix} 2 & -1 \\ -7 & 4 \end{pmatrix}$

2. $\begin{pmatrix} 2 & -3 \\ -7 & 11 \end{pmatrix}$

3. $\begin{pmatrix} -2 & 3 \\ -7 & 10 \end{pmatrix}$

4. $\begin{pmatrix} 7 & -5 \\ -4 & 3 \end{pmatrix}$

5. $\begin{pmatrix} 7 & -4 \\ -12 & 7 \end{pmatrix}$

6. $\begin{pmatrix} 2 & -1 \\ -1 & 1 \end{pmatrix}$

EXERCISE 8f
(p. 138)

Before Number 16, ask the pupils to try to find the inverse of, say, $\begin{pmatrix} 2 & 1 \\ 4 & 2 \end{pmatrix}$ and discuss again the fact that division by zero is impossible—hence no inverse.

1. $\begin{pmatrix} 1\frac{1}{2} & -1 \\ -4 & 3 \end{pmatrix}$

2. $\begin{pmatrix} \frac{1}{3} & -\frac{2}{3} \\ -1 & 3 \end{pmatrix}$

3. $\begin{pmatrix} 1\frac{1}{2} & -\frac{1}{2} \\ -2\frac{1}{2} & 1 \end{pmatrix}$

4. $\begin{pmatrix} \frac{1}{3} & \frac{2}{3} \\ -\frac{1}{3} & \frac{1}{3} \end{pmatrix}$

5. $\begin{pmatrix} \frac{1}{2} & 0 \\ 0 & \frac{1}{3} \end{pmatrix}$

6. $\begin{pmatrix} 4 & -1 \\ -5\frac{1}{2} & 1\frac{1}{2} \end{pmatrix}$

7. $\begin{pmatrix} 4 & 3 \\ 5 & 4 \end{pmatrix}$

8. $\begin{pmatrix} 4 & -3 \\ -5 & 4 \end{pmatrix}$

9. $\begin{pmatrix} 1 & 1 \\ \frac{1}{2} & \frac{3}{4} \end{pmatrix}$

10. $\begin{pmatrix} -1 & 1 \\ 3\frac{1}{2} & -3 \end{pmatrix}$

11. $\begin{pmatrix} -1 & 2 \\ 2\frac{1}{2} & -4\frac{1}{2} \end{pmatrix}$

12. $\begin{pmatrix} -\frac{1}{5} & \frac{1}{5} \\ \frac{1}{5} & \frac{4}{5} \end{pmatrix}$

13. $\begin{pmatrix} -1 & 1 \\ 2 & -1\frac{1}{2} \end{pmatrix}$

14. $\begin{pmatrix} -1 & -1\frac{1}{3} \\ -1 & -1 \end{pmatrix}$

15. $\begin{pmatrix} -3 & 2 \\ 4 & -2\frac{1}{2} \end{pmatrix}$

16. a) Yes   b) No   c) Yes
17. a) Yes   b) Yes   c) Yes

18. $\begin{pmatrix} 1 & -1 \\ -1 & 1\frac{1}{5} \end{pmatrix}$

19. No inverse

20. $\begin{pmatrix} \frac{1}{5} & 0 \\ 0 & \frac{1}{5} \end{pmatrix}$

21. $\begin{pmatrix} -4 & 7 \\ 3 & -5 \end{pmatrix}$

22. $\begin{pmatrix} 2 & -1 \\ -3 & 1\frac{2}{3} \end{pmatrix}$

23. No inverse

EXERCISE 8g
(p. 140)

1. 1, $\begin{pmatrix} 2 & -3 \\ -3 & 5 \end{pmatrix}$

2. 2, $\begin{pmatrix} 1\frac{1}{2} & -1 \\ -1 & 1 \end{pmatrix}$

3. I

4. $\begin{pmatrix} 16 & 19 \\ 10 & 12 \end{pmatrix}$

5. $\begin{pmatrix} 6 & -9\frac{1}{2} \\ -5 & 8 \end{pmatrix}$

6. $\begin{pmatrix} 6 & -5 \\ -9\frac{1}{2} & 8 \end{pmatrix}$

7. $\begin{pmatrix} 6 & -9\frac{1}{2} \\ -5 & 8 \end{pmatrix}$

8. $\begin{pmatrix} 34 & 21 \\ 21 & 13 \end{pmatrix}$

9. $\begin{pmatrix} 13 & -21 \\ -21 & 34 \end{pmatrix}$

10. $\begin{pmatrix} 13 & -21 \\ -21 & 34 \end{pmatrix}$

11. $\begin{pmatrix} 2 & 1 \\ -3\frac{1}{2} & -1\frac{1}{2} \end{pmatrix}$

12. $\begin{pmatrix} -2\frac{1}{2} & 4 \\ -2 & 3 \end{pmatrix}$

EXERCISE 8h
(p. 142)

The formula for finding the value of |A| is not essential and none of the questions in the rest of this chapter depends upon it.

1. 9
2. 17
3. 0
4. 19

5. −14
6. 10
7. −1
8. −8

9. 9
10. 5
11. 5
12. −9

EXERCISE 8i
(p. 143)
Solution of simultaneous equations by elimination demands that decisions are made at several stages. Pupils may notice that using matrices to solve simultaneous equations is not as neat as the elimination method and generally takes longer. This is a good time to explain that, because no decisions have to be made when using matrices, it is an ideal method for computer programming.

1. $x + 2y = 3$
$\quad 3x + 2y = 5$
2. $4x + 2y = 12$
$\quad 5x + 3y = 15$

3. $9x + 2y = 24$
$\quad 4x + y = 11$
4. $6p - q = -8$
$\quad 2p + q = 0$

5. $\begin{pmatrix} 3 & 2 \\ 1 & 1 \end{pmatrix}\begin{pmatrix} x \\ y \end{pmatrix} = \begin{pmatrix} 8 \\ 3 \end{pmatrix}$

6. $\begin{pmatrix} 4 & -3 \\ 2 & 1 \end{pmatrix}\begin{pmatrix} x \\ y \end{pmatrix} = \begin{pmatrix} 1 \\ 3 \end{pmatrix}$

7. $\begin{pmatrix} 4 & 3 \\ 5 & 4 \end{pmatrix}\begin{pmatrix} x \\ y \end{pmatrix} = \begin{pmatrix} 5 \\ 6 \end{pmatrix}$

8. $\begin{pmatrix} 3 & -2 \\ 1 & -1 \end{pmatrix}\begin{pmatrix} x \\ y \end{pmatrix} = \begin{pmatrix} 1 \\ 0 \end{pmatrix}$

9. $\begin{pmatrix} 7 & -2 \\ 3 & 4 \end{pmatrix}\begin{pmatrix} x \\ y \end{pmatrix} = \begin{pmatrix} 3 \\ 11 \end{pmatrix}$

10. $\begin{pmatrix} 5 & 1 \\ 4 & -3 \end{pmatrix}\begin{pmatrix} x \\ y \end{pmatrix} = \begin{pmatrix} -8 \\ -14 \end{pmatrix}$

EXERCISE 8j
(p. 145)
1. $x = 1$, $y = 2$
2. $x = 2$, $y = 3$
3. $x = 1$, $y = -1$
4. $x = 2$, $y = -1$
5. $x = 3$, $y = 0$

6. $x = 1$, $y = 2$
7. $x = 4$, $y = 2$
8. $x = 1$, $y = -2$
9. $x = 4$, $y = 2$
10. $p = 1$, $q = 1$
11. $s = -2$, $t = 3$

12. $\begin{pmatrix} 1 & 1 \\ 1 & 2 \end{pmatrix}\begin{pmatrix} x \\ y \end{pmatrix} = \begin{pmatrix} 2 \\ 3 \end{pmatrix}$; $x = 1$, $y = 1$

13. $\begin{pmatrix} 4 & -1 \\ 1 & 1 \end{pmatrix}\begin{pmatrix} x \\ y \end{pmatrix} = \begin{pmatrix} 5 \\ 5 \end{pmatrix}$; $x = 2$, $y = 3$

14. $\begin{pmatrix} 5 & 4 \\ 1 & 1 \end{pmatrix}\begin{pmatrix} x \\ y \end{pmatrix} = \begin{pmatrix} 1 \\ 0 \end{pmatrix}$; $x = 1$, $y = -1$

15. $\begin{pmatrix} 2 & 3 \\ 3 & 5 \end{pmatrix}\begin{pmatrix} x \\ y \end{pmatrix} = \begin{pmatrix} 15 \\ 23 \end{pmatrix}$; $x = 6$, $y = 1$

16. $\begin{pmatrix} 9 & 2 \\ 3 & 1 \end{pmatrix}\begin{pmatrix} x \\ y \end{pmatrix} = \begin{pmatrix} 11 \\ 5 \end{pmatrix}$; $x = \frac{1}{3}$, $y = 4$

17. $\begin{pmatrix} 2 & 3 \\ 3 & 2 \end{pmatrix}\begin{pmatrix} x \\ y \end{pmatrix} = \begin{pmatrix} 7 \\ 8 \end{pmatrix}$; $x = 2$, $y = 1$

18. $\begin{pmatrix} 5 & 2 \\ 3 & -1 \end{pmatrix}\begin{pmatrix} x \\ y \end{pmatrix} = \begin{pmatrix} 16 \\ 3 \end{pmatrix}$; $x = 2$, $y = 3$

19. $\begin{pmatrix} 1 & 4 \\ 2 & 3 \end{pmatrix}\begin{pmatrix} x \\ y \end{pmatrix} = \begin{pmatrix} 11 \\ 7 \end{pmatrix}$; $x = -1$, $y = 3$

20. Determinant is zero so there is no inverse.
21. Determinant is zero so there is no inverse.

EXERCISE 8k
(p. 147)

1. $\begin{pmatrix} 5 & 6 \\ -3 & 0 \end{pmatrix}$

2. $\begin{pmatrix} 7 & 2 \\ -3 & 2 \end{pmatrix}$

3. $\begin{pmatrix} 15 & 19 \\ 9 & 9 \end{pmatrix}$

4. $\begin{pmatrix} -5 & -6 \\ 3 & 0 \end{pmatrix}$

5. $\begin{pmatrix} 2 & 1\frac{1}{2} \\ 1 & \frac{1}{2} \end{pmatrix}$

6. $\begin{pmatrix} 3 & -6 \\ 0 & 3 \end{pmatrix}$

7. $\begin{pmatrix} 3 & -1 \\ -5 & 1 \end{pmatrix}$

8. $\begin{pmatrix} -\frac{1}{2} & 1\frac{1}{2} \\ 1 & -2 \end{pmatrix}$.

EXERCISE 8l
(p. 147)

1. $\begin{pmatrix} 5 & 4 & 3 \\ 10 & -8 & 4 \end{pmatrix}$

2. $\begin{pmatrix} 1 & 3\frac{1}{2} \\ 1\frac{1}{2} & -\frac{1}{2} \end{pmatrix}$

3. 24

4. $\begin{pmatrix} \frac{4}{7} & -\frac{3}{7} \\ -\frac{3}{7} & \frac{4}{7} \end{pmatrix}$

5. (-9)

6. $\begin{pmatrix} 13 & 33 \\ 6 & 22 \end{pmatrix}$

EXERCISE 8m
(p. 148)

1. $\begin{pmatrix} 5 & 3 \\ -1 & 4 \end{pmatrix}$

2. 2

3. $\begin{pmatrix} 1 & 1 \\ 2 & 3 \end{pmatrix}$

4. $\begin{pmatrix} 3 \\ -1 \end{pmatrix}$

5. $(6 \ 10)$

6. $(3 \ -1\frac{1}{2})$

Codes: The following is a fun way of using matrices and gives extra practice in the use of inverses. It does take a long time though, especially with those pupils who are careless!

We can use a 2×2 matrix to code a message and we can use its inverse for decoding. Choose a matrix with a determinant of 1 so that the entries in the inverse are whole numbers: for example $\begin{pmatrix} 2 & 1 \\ 1 & 1 \end{pmatrix}$ has as its inverse $\begin{pmatrix} 1 & -1 \\ -1 & 2 \end{pmatrix}$.

Give to each letter of the message a number according to its position in the alphabet.

$$\begin{array}{cccccc} G & O & A & W & A & Y \\ 7 & 15 & 1 & 23 & 1 & 25 \end{array}$$

Make the number of letters up to a multiple of 4 by adding "A"s.

$$\begin{array}{cccccccc} G & O & A & W & A & Y & A & A \\ 7 & 15 & 1 & 23 & 1 & 25 & 1 & 1 \end{array}$$

Now we can form two 2×2 matrices from these numbers, i.e. $\begin{pmatrix} 7 & 15 \\ 1 & 23 \end{pmatrix}$ and $\begin{pmatrix} 1 & 25 \\ 1 & 1 \end{pmatrix}$.

Premultiply each by the coding matrix.

$$\begin{pmatrix} 2 & 1 \\ 1 & 1 \end{pmatrix}\begin{pmatrix} 7 & 15 \\ 1 & 23 \end{pmatrix} = \begin{pmatrix} 15 & 53 \\ 8 & 38 \end{pmatrix}$$

$$\begin{pmatrix} 2 & 1 \\ 1 & 1 \end{pmatrix}\begin{pmatrix} 1 & 25 \\ 1 & 1 \end{pmatrix} = \begin{pmatrix} 3 & 51 \\ 2 & 26 \end{pmatrix}$$

The coded message is 15, 53, 8, 38, 3, 51, 2, 26.
To decode the message we form matrices again from the coded message and use the decoder, that is, the inverse matrix. This gives the original numbers.

$$\begin{pmatrix} 1 & -1 \\ -1 & 2 \end{pmatrix}\begin{pmatrix} 15 & 53 \\ 8 & 38 \end{pmatrix} = \begin{pmatrix} 7 & 15 \\ 1 & 23 \end{pmatrix} \text{ and } \begin{pmatrix} 1 & -1 \\ -1 & 2 \end{pmatrix}\begin{pmatrix} 3 & 51 \\ 2 & 26 \end{pmatrix} = \begin{pmatrix} 1 & 25 \\ 1 & 1 \end{pmatrix}$$

The following messages have been coded using the given matrices.

1. GOODBYE $\begin{pmatrix} 2 & -1 \\ 3 & -1 \end{pmatrix}$ $-1, 26, 6, 41, -1, 49, 1, 74$

2. HAPPY BIRTHDAY $\begin{pmatrix} 3 & 4 \\ 2 & 3 \end{pmatrix}$ 88, 67, 64, 50, 111, 78, 77, 58, 76, 28, 52, 19, 79, 7, 53, 5

3. JACK AND JILL $\begin{pmatrix} 3 & 5 \\ 1 & 2 \end{pmatrix}$ 45, 58, 16, 23, 23, 92, 9, 34, 87, 41, 33, 14

4. GEOMETRY $\begin{pmatrix} 4 & 7 \\ 1 & 2 \end{pmatrix}$ 133, 111, 37, 31, 146, 255, 41, 70

5. HULLO $\begin{pmatrix} 2 & 1 \\ 1 & 1 \end{pmatrix}$ 28, 54, 20, 33, 31, 3, 16, 2

CHAPTER 9 Areas

EXERCISE 9a
(p. 149)
Revises areas of rectangles, parallelograms and triangles.

1. $20\,cm^2$
2. $10\,cm^2$
3. $17\,cm^2$
4. $19.35\,cm^2$
5. 12 sq. units
6. 30 sq. units
7. 12 sq. units
8. 16 sq. units
9. $24\frac{1}{2}$ sq. units
10. 4 cm
11. $450\,mm^2$
12. 5 cm
13. 5 m, $25\,m^2$
14. 4 cm
15. a) $17.5\,cm^2$ b) 5.83 cm
16. a) $12\,cm^2$ b) 3.43 cm
17. a) $40\,cm^2$ b) 6.67 cm
18. a) $7\,cm^2$ b) 2 cm

EXERCISE 9b
(p. 151)
Revises areas of compound shapes.

1. $60\,cm^2$
2. $40\,cm^2$
3. $30\,cm^2$
4. $45\,cm^2$
5. $135\,cm^2$
6. $27.75\,cm^2$

EXERCISE 9c
(p. 153)
It is worth showing, by expanding $\frac{1}{2}(p+q) \times h$, that this is an alternative way of writing $\frac{1}{2}ph + \frac{1}{2}qh$, because "common factors" have not been covered at this stage.

1. $42\,cm^2$
2. $94.5\,cm^2$
3. $21\,cm^2$
4. $8.75\,cm^2$

5. 30 sq. units   **8.** 16 sq. units
6. 33 sq. units   **9.** 84 sq. units
7. 56 sq. units   **10.** 47 sq. units

EXERCISE 9d
(p. 155) This and the next exercise can be omitted, or used for discussion only.

1. Area of each parallelogram is 35 cm²
2. Area of each triangle is 28 cm²
3. Each parallelogram has a base of length 4 units and height of 3 units. The areas are each equal to 12 sq. units
4. Each base is 6 units long. Each height is 3 units. The areas are each equal to 9 sq. units
8. Ratio of heights is 4:5:7:9. Ratio of areas is 4:5:7:9. The ratio of areas is equal to the ratio of heights
9. The y coordinate of D is 9 (or -7 if drawn below the x-axis)
10. The y coordinate of E is 3 (or -1 if drawn below the x-axis)

EXERCISE 9e
(p. 157) Use for discussion with everyone. Only the most able should attempt these on their own. It is particularly difficult to produce a *reasoned* answer for Number 11. For Numbers 12 and 13 pupils need to be reminded how to construct parallel lines.

7. 12 cm   **8.** 2:1   **9.** 14 cm   **10.** 8 cm   **11.** 30°
12. △BEC = 27 cm², △DEC = 12 cm²   **13.** 132°   **14.** 6 cm

CHAPTER 10   Angles in Circles

In Exercise 10a a movement starts towards a more formal and non-numerical treatment of geometry. The first section revises the basic facts and begins the progression towards a reasoned answer. The proof that the sum of the interior angles of a triangle is 180° can be used to demonstrate what can be reasoned from a few known facts. It can also be used to demonstrate what is acceptable as a reason. However the emphasis throughout this book is still on the intuitive recognition of facts.

Geometry is put on a more formal and non-numerical basis in Book 4A with an introduction to the deductive nature of Euclidian Geometry.

EXERCISE 10a
(p. 163) Numbers 15–20 are non-numerical and several examples should be used for discussion before pupils attempt them on their own. It is sensible to accept, as reasons, any facts that they know, e.g. in Number 4 they may use the fact that opposite angles of a parallelogram are equal. Some discussion is also necessary on naming angles when there is more than one angle at a vertex. Either the angle must be clearly marked on the diagram with a small letter or three letters have to be used.

1. 70°   **5.** 45
2. 110°   **6.** 55°
3. 60°   **7.** 125°
4. 70°   **8.** 66°

    9. $d = 75°, e = 65°, f = 140°$
  10. $p. = 60°, q = 60°, r = 120°, s = 60°$
  11. $k = 30°, l = 30°, m = 30°, n = 60°$
  12. $g = 24°, h = 156°, i = 74°$
  13. $w = 73°, x = 34°, y = 34°, z = 73°$
  14. $d = 64°, e = 64°, f = 116°, g = 116°, h = 64°$

EXERCISE 10b   **1.** Yes   **6.** No
(p. 168)   **2.** No   **7.** Yes
            3. Yes   **8.** No
            4. No   **9.** Yes
            5. Yes   **10.** Yes

EXERCISE 10c   **1.** Reflection in x-axis; Yes
(p. 170)   **2.** Rotation of 90° anticlockwise about 0; Yes
            3. Enlargement, scale factor 2, centre $(-4, 0)$; No
            4. Translation $\begin{pmatrix} -3 \\ -2 \end{pmatrix}$; Yes
            5. Reflection in y-axis; Yes
            6. Enlargement, scale factor $\frac{1}{2}$, centre $(0, 0)$; No
            7. Rotation of 90° clockwise about $(5, 2)$; Yes
            8. Translation $\begin{pmatrix} -3 \\ -2 \end{pmatrix}$; Yes

Many pupils have problems with circle questions because they do not have a clear understanding of a) the meaning of "subtends", b) what a segment of a circle is. The next two exercises attempt to remedy this.

EXERCISE 10d   **1.** AB, AC, AD, BC, BD, CD. Yes, AC.
(p. 174)

2.   **4.**

3.   **5.**

EXERCISE 10e
(p. 176)

1. Minor arc DC
2. Minor arc BC
3. $A\hat{C}B$, $A\hat{D}B$
4. $B\hat{A}C$, $B\hat{D}C$
5. DA
6. AB

7. Minor arc BE
8. Minor arc CD
9. CE
10. DB

11. a) $A\hat{C}B$, $A\hat{E}B$
    b) $B\hat{A}C$, $B\hat{E}C$
12. a) $A\hat{B}E$, $A\hat{C}E$, $A\hat{D}E$
    b) $C\hat{D}E$, $C\hat{A}E$, $C\hat{B}E$

Experimental Work Some teachers (and pupils!) may find the experimental work detailed below quite useful. The work may be illustrated by the teacher or, better still, pupils should be encouraged to make their own models using, for example, covers from old exercise books.

As an introduction you may choose to go through all the experiments (results) at one sitting, but to repeat them as each new fact is taught. Four experiments are listed, three of them yielding the five facts used in this chapter. The alternate segment result will not be used until Book 4A, but it is certainly worth a mention here since the model illustrates it so nicely.

All the results can be confirmed by diagrams and measurements.

Preparing the Model You require two pieces of cardboard or stiff paper, preferably of different colours. The first should be a square of side approximately 18 cm and the other a rectangle measuring 20 cm by 12 cm.

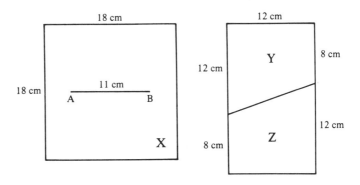

In the square piece cut a slot AB, 11 cm long, near the middle of the card. Cut the second piece along the line shown in the diagram to give two identical trapeziums Y and Z.

Experiment 1: (illustrating "angles in the same segment" and "opposite angles of a cyclic quadrilateral" result).

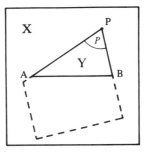

Take the trapezium Y and mark the acute angle P. Push P through the slot AB from behind, until the trapezium will not go any further. Mark with a dot the position of P on the square X.

Rotate the card Y into another position (again making sure that Y fills the slot) and mark the new position of P. Do this several times marking each position of P as shown below.

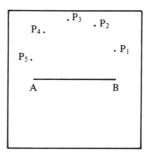

Now mark the obtuse angle of Y with the letter Q.

Push Y through the slot from behind as shown in the diagram and mark the position of Q. Rotate Y to give several positions of Q.

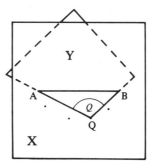

Take Y out and note that all the marked points look as though they lie on a circle. The different positions of P seem to lie on a major arc and the different positions of Q on a minor arc.

Card X should now look like this:

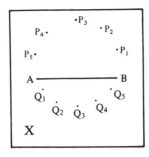

Experiment 2:   (illustrating "angle at centre" result).

Take Y and Z and place them together as shown below (you might find it useful to sellotape them together).

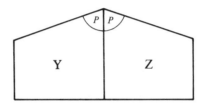

Now push them together through the slot AB from behind, keeping the edges of Y and Z parallel to the edges of the rectangle as indicated. Mark O as shown.

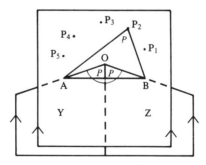

Take Y and Z out of the slot. With centre O and radius OA draw the major arc AB which will be seen to pass through P_1, P_2, . . .

Experiment 3:   (illustrating "angle in a semicircle" result).

Turn the square card over to use the opposite side. Use one of the right angles from Y or Z and place it upwards through the slot AB from behind. Mark the position of the right angle R. Repeat this with R in several different positions.

Now place the right angle downwards through **AB** from behind and mark several additional positions of R.

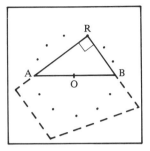

Remove the trapezium and find the midpoint O of AB. Centre O, radius OA, draw a circle.

Experiment 4:   ("alternate segment" result).

Fig. 1.

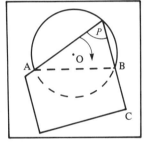

Fig. 2.

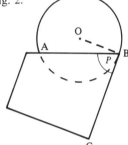

Place one trapezium on the circle obtained in the first experiment such that it gives one position for P. This is shown in Figure 1. Now rotate the trapezium downwards about A so that P moves along the circle towards B. Figure 2 shows the position when AP coincides with AB. OB is a radius and you can see that the side CB on the trapezium has only one point of contact with the circle, that is at B.

CB is a tangent to the circle at B

Since $A\hat{P}B = A\hat{B}C$ this experiment shows that:

the angle between a tangent and a chord drawn at the point of contact, is equal to the angle in the alternate segment.

EXERCISE 10f Answers depend on pupils' drawings but in each question the angles should be
(p. 176)   equal.

EXERCISE 10g **1.** $h = 38°$ **3.** $x = 33° = y$
(p. 177)   **2.** $i = 39°, j = 46°$ **4.** $p = 72°, q = 57°$

                  5. $l = 100°$ **7.** $w = 57°, x = 123°$
                  6. $x = 108°, y = 26°$ **8.** $c = 114°$

40   *ST(P) Mathematics 3A*

EXERCISE 10h Answers depend on pupils' drawings but in each question $y = 2x$.
(p. 179)

EXERCISE 10i **1.** $d = 80°$ **3.** $f = 114°$ **5.** $g = 98°$ **7.** $l = 132°$
(p. 180)   **2.** $e = 64°$ **4.** $i = 38°$ **6.** $h = 32°$ **8.** $m = 102°$

EXERCISE 10j Answers depend on pupils' drawings but in each question $p+q = 180°$.
(p. 182)

EXERCISE 10k **1.** $d = 108°$ **3.** $f = 103°$ **5.** $l = 131°$ **7.** $g = 121°, h = 68°$
(p. 183)   **2.** $e = 84°$ **4.** $k = 115°$ **6.** $m = 87°, n = 112°$ **8.** $i = 110°, j = 50°$

EXERCISE 10l Answers depend on pupils' drawings but the conclusions should be:
(p. 185)
    1. $p = q$ **3.** $s = r$ **5.** $y = 100°$ **7.** $p = 54°, q = 76°$
    2. $v = u$ **4.** $x = w$ **6.** $z = 109°$ **8.** $r = 126°, s = 83°$

EXERCISE 10m **1.** $a = 44°$ **4.** $b = 78°$
(p. 186)   **2.** $c = 60°, d = 46°$ **5.** $e = 34°, f = 52°$
    3. $g = 116°$ **6.** $h = 72°$
    7. $l = 154°, m = 40°, n = 37°$
    8. $r = 110°, s = 122°$
    9. $x = 30°, y = 58°, z = 88°$
    10. $c = 25°, d = 25°, e = 50°$
    11. $h = 116°, i = 32°$
    12. $l = 126°, m = 63°, n = 117°$
    13. $u = 34°, v = 68°, w = 56°, x = 56°$
    14. $k = 62°, l = 56°, m = 124°, n = 16°$

EXERCISE 10n **1.** $d = 90° = e$ **2.** $f = 90° = g$ **3.** $h = 90° = i$
(p. 187)

EXERCISE 10p **1.** $d = 90°, e = 53°$ **4.** $l = 90°, m = 61°$
(p. 188)   **2.** $f = 90°, g = 45°$ **5.** $j = 90°, k = 55°$
    3. $h = 90°, i = 26°$ **6.** $p = 90°, q = 38°$

    7. $r = 90°, s = 52°, t = 90°, u = 43°$
    8. $d = 90°, e = 45°, f = 90°, g = 18°$
    9. $c = 90°, d = 58°, e = 32°$
    10. $v = 90°, w = 47°, x = 90°, y = 51°$
    11. $j = 90°, k = 33°, l = 33°, m = 57°$
    12. $f = 45°, g = 58°, h = 45°, i = 32°$

EXERCISE 10q **1.** $d = 106°$

(p. 190)   **2.** $e = f = 38°$

3. $d = 34°, e = 68°$

4. $x = 75°, y = 15°, z = 132°$

5. $p = 36° = q, r = 39°$
6. $x = 112°, y = 68°, z = 112°$
7. $g = 54°, h = 120°$
8. $d = 37°, e = 53°, f = 57°, g = 33°$

CHAPTER 11 Algebraic Products

Much of the work in this chapter can be done as oral classwork.

EXERCISE 11a **1.** $2x + 2$

(p. 192)   **2.** $3x - 3$

   3. $4x + 12$

4. $5a + 20$

5. $3b + 21$

6. $3 - 3a$

7. $5 - 5b$

8. $6a - 2$

9. $8 + 12b$

10. $5ab - 5ac$
11. $4ab - 8ac$
12. $6a^2 + 3ab$

13. $15xy + 5xz$
14. $16xy + 12yz$
15. $6np - 10nq$

16. $16rt - 8rs$
17. $3ab - 15ac$
18. $12xy + 8xz$

EXERCISE 11b The suggested order for multiplying the terms in the two brackets gives lines which

(p. 193)   some pupils see as forming a face. Two lines give the eyebrows, while the other two
form the nose and chin.
Some teachers may prefer a different order, e.g.

$$(\overparen{a + b})(c + d) = ac + ad + bc + bd$$

1. $ac + ad + bc + bd$
2. $ps + pt + qs + qt$
3. $2ac + 4ad + bc + 2bd$
4. $5xz + 15x + 2yz + 6y$
5. $xz - 4x + yz - 4y$

6. $ac + ad - bc - bd$
7. $xy + xz + y^2 + yz$
8. $6ac + 2ad + 3bc + bd$
9. $5xz + 10x + 4yz + 8y$
10. $15x - 3xz - 10y + 2yz$

11. $2ps - 3pt + 2qs - 3qt$
12. $ac - ad - 2bc + 2bd$
13. $6uw - 30ur - 5vw + 25vr$
14. $6ac - 9ad + 8bc - 12bd$
15. $9xz + 6x + 6yz + 4y$

16. $12pr - 9ps - 4qr + 3qs$
17. $9ac + 12ad - 12bc - 16bd$
18. $21x - 14xz - 6y + 4yz$
19. $10ac - 4a + 5bc - 2b$
20. $15a - 10ad - 12b + 8bd$

EXERCISE 11c With other than above average pupils it is probably wise to write down the four

(p. 193)   terms obtained by multiplying the brackets, and then to collect like terms as a
separate step.

1. $x^2 + 7x + 12$
2. $x^2 + 6x + 8$

3. $x^2 + 7x + 6$
4. $x^2 + 7x + 10$

5. $x^2 + 11x + 24$
6. $a^2 + 9a + 20$
7. $b^2 + 9b + 14$

8. $c^2 + 10c + 24$
9. $p^2 + 15p + 36$
10. $q^2 + 17q + 70$

11. $x^2 - 5x + 6$
12. $x^2 - 12x + 35$
13. $a^2 - 10a + 16$
14. $x^2 - 13x + 30$
15. $b^2 - 10b + 25$

16. $x^2 - 7x + 12$
17. $x^2 - 12x + 32$
18. $b^2 - 6b + 8$
19. $a^2 - 8a + 16$
20. $p^2 - 15p + 56$

21. $x^2 + x - 6$
22. $x^2 + x - 20$
23. $x^2 - 3x - 28$
24. $a^2 - 7a - 30$
25. $p^2 - 25$

26. $x^2 + 5x - 14$
27. $x^2 + x - 30$
28. $x^2 + 9x - 10$
29. $b^2 - 15b + 56$
30. $z^2 - 13z + 12$

EXERCISE 11d The value of setting out as given in the text will become apparent when factorising
(p. 195) is considered in the next chapter.

1. $x^2 + 9x + 20$
2. $a^2 + 7a + 10$
3. $x^2 - 9x + 20$
4. $a^2 - 7a + 10$

5. $x^2 + 14x + 48$
6. $a^2 + 17a + 70$
7. $x^2 - 14x + 48$
8. $a^2 - 17a + 70$

9. $a^2 - 3a - 10$
10. $y^2 - 3y - 18$
11. $z^2 - 6z - 40$
12. $p^2 - 3p - 40$

13. $a^2 - 3a - 70$
14. $y^2 + 8y - 20$
15. $z^2 - 11z - 12$
16. $p^2 - 11p - 26$

17. $x^2 - 6x + 5$
18. $b^2 + 16b + 63$
19. $a^2 - 16$
20. $r^2 - 12r - 28$

21. $p^2 + 14p + 24$
22. $t^2 - 7t - 60$
23. $c^2 + 3c - 40$
24. $x^2 - 25$

EXERCISE 11e
(p. 196)

1. $2x^2 + 3x + 1$
2. $5x^2 + 12x + 4$
3. $5x^2 + 17x + 6$
4. $3x^2 + 19x + 20$

5. $3x^2 + 5x + 2$
6. $3x^2 + 11x + 6$
7. $4x^2 + 7x + 3$
8. $7x^2 + 23x + 6$

9. $6x^2 + 13x + 6$
10. $12x^2 - 25x + 12$
11. $10x^2 - 3x - 18$
12. $21a^2 - 58a + 21$

13. $10x^2 + 31x + 15$
14. $21x^2 - 20x + 4$
15. $12x^2 - 5x - 2$
16. $6b^2 - 5b - 25$

17. $4a^2 - 9$
18. $9b^2 - 49$
19. $49y^2 - 25$
20. $20a^2 + a - 12$

21. $16x^2 - 9$
22. $25y^2 - 4$
23. $9x^2 - 1$
24. $16x^2 - 8x - 35$

25. $6x^2 + 5x + 1$

26. $-5x^2 + 8x + 4$

27. $-6x^2 + 19x - 3$

28. $-35a^2 + 29a - 6$

29. $8 + 10x - 3x^2$

30. $4x^2 + 7x - 15$

31. $15x^2 + 26x + 8$

32. $-14x^2 + 13x + 12$

33. $-20x^2 + 27x - 9$

34. $12 - p - p^2$

35. $x^2 - 3x - 10$

36. $4x^2 + 9x - 9$

Better pupils would be expected to remember and use the screened results. Some teachers may like to illustrate these results geometrically, for example:

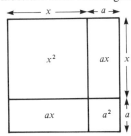

Area of whole $= (x+a)^2$

Total area of separate parts $= x^2 + ax + ax + a^2$

$\qquad\qquad\qquad\qquad\quad = x^2 + 2ax + a^2$

Therefore $\qquad (x+a)^2 = x^2 + 2ax + a^2$

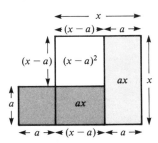

Area of whole $=$ area of large square $+$ area of small square

$\qquad\qquad\quad = x^2 + a^2$

Area of whole also $= (x-a)^2 + ax + ax$

Therefore $\qquad\qquad (x-a)^2 + 2ax = x^2 + a^2$

i.e. $\qquad\qquad\qquad (x-a)^2 = x^2 - 2ax + a^2$

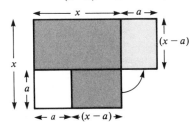

Area shaded is $x^2 - a^2$

The rectangle measuring $(x+a)$ by $(x-a)$ has an equal area which is $(x+a)(x-a)$

Therefore $\qquad\qquad\qquad x^2 - a^2 = (x+a)(x-a)$

EXERCISE 11f
(p. 198)

1. $x^2 + 2x + 1$
2. $x^2 + 4x + 4$
3. $a^2 + 6a + 9$
4. $b^2 + 8b + 16$

5. $t^2 + 20t + 100$
6. $x^2 + 24x + 144$
7. $x^2 + 16x + 64$
8. $p^2 + 14p + 49$

9. $x^2 + 2xy + y^2$
10. $y^2 + 2yz + z^2$
11. $c^2 + 2cd + d^2$
12. $m^2 + 2mn + n^2$

13. $p^2 + 2pq + q^2$
14. $a^2 + 2ab + b^2$
15. $e^2 + 2ef + f^2$
16. $u^2 + 2uv + v^2$

17. $4x^2 + 4x + 1$
18. $16b^2 + 8b + 1$
19. $25x^2 + 20x + 4$
20. $36c^2 + 12c + 1$

21. $9a^2 + 6a + 1$
22. $4x^2 + 20x + 25$
23. $9a^2 + 24a + 16$
24. $16y^2 + 24y + 9$

25. $x^2 + 4xy + 4y^2$
26. $9x^2 + 6xy + y^2$
27. $4x^2 + 20xy + 25y^2$
28. $9a^2 + 12ab + 4b^2$

29. $9a^2 + 6ab + b^2$
30. $p^2 + 8pq + 16q^2$
31. $49x^2 + 28xy + 4y^2$
32. $9s^2 + 24st + 16t^2$

33. $x^2 - 4x + 4$
34. $x^2 - 12x + 36$
35. $a^2 - 20a + 100$
36. $x^2 - 2xy + y^2$

37. $x^2 - 6x + 9$
38. $x^2 - 14x + 49$
39. $a^2 - 2ab + b^2$
40. $u^2 - 2uv + v^2$

41. $9x^2 - 6x + 1$
42. $25z^2 - 10z + 1$
43. $100a^2 - 180a + 81$
44. $16x^2 - 24x + 9$

45. $4a^2 - 4a + 1$
46. $16y^2 - 8y + 1$
47. $49b^2 - 28b + 4$
48. $25x^2 - 30x + 9$

49. $4y^2 - 4yx + x^2$
50. $25x^2 - 10xy + y^2$
51. $9m^2 - 12mn + 4n^2$
52. $49x^2 - 42xy + 9y^2$

53. $a^2 - 6ab + 9b^2$
54. $m^2 - 16mn + 64n^2$
55. $25a^2 - 20ab + 4b^2$
56. $9p^2 - 30pq + 25q^2$

EXERCISE 11g
(p. 200)

1. $x^2 - 16$
2. $b^2 - 36$
3. $c^2 - 9$
4. $x^2 - 144$

5. $x^2 - 25$
6. $a^2 - 49$
7. $q^2 - 100$
8. $x^2 - 64$

9. $4x^2 - 1$
10. $9x^2 - 1$
11. $49a^2 - 4$
12. $25a^2 - 16$

13. $25x^2 - 1$
14. $4a^2 - 9$
15. $100m^2 - 1$
16. $36a^2 - 25$

17. $9x^2 - 16y^2$
18. $4a^2 - 25b^2$
19. $1 - 4a^2$
20. $49y^2 - 9z^2$
21. $100a^2 - 81b^2$

22. $25a^2 - 16b^2$
23. $1 - 9x^2$
24. $9 - 25x^2$
25. $25m^2 - 64n^2$
26. $36p^2 - 49q^2$

EXERCISE 11h
(p. 201)

1. $2x^2 + 9x + 12$
2. $2x^2 + 9x + 2$
3. $x^2 + 15x + 32$
4. $a^2 - 9a + 36$
5. $2a^2 - 10a - 3$

6. $x^2 + 13x + 25$
7. $x^2 - 2x - 21$
8. $x^2 - 2x - 23$
9. $16x^2 + 6x - 10$
10. $12x^2 + 8x - 20$

11. $x^2y^2 - 6xy + 9$
12. $25 - 10yz + y^2z^2$
13. $x^2y^2 + 8xy + 16$
14. $9p^2q^2 + 48pq + 64$
15. $a^2 - 2abc + b^2c^2$

16. $a^2b^2 - 4ab + 4$
17. $36 - 12pq + p^2q^2$
18. $m^2n^2 + 6mn + 9$
19. $u^2v^2 - 4uvw + 4w^2$

Summary: This could prove very useful for periodic revision using home grown examples or the mixed exercises that follow.

EXERCISE 11i
(p. 203)

1. $5x + 10$
2. $24pq - 16pr$
3. $6a^2 - 13ab - 5b^2$
4. $12x^2 - 17x - 5$
5. $x^2 + 16x + 60$

6. $x^2 - 20x + 96$
7. $16y^2 - 16y - 21$
8. $16y^2 - 81$
9. $25x^2 + 20x + 4$
10. $4a^2 - 28ab + 49b^2$

EXERCISE 11j
(p. 204)

1. $8 - 20x$
2. $16a - 24a^2$
3. $12a^2 - 35a - 33$
4. $x^2 + 2x - 99$
5. $-20x^2 - 48x + 5$

6. $y^2 + 4yz + 4z^2$
7. $36y^2 + 24yz - 5z^2$
8. $16a^2 + 8a + 1$
9. $25a^2 - 70a + 49$
10. $36z^2 - 156zy + 169y^2$

EXERCISE 11k
(p. 204)

1. $6 - 3a$
2. $8ab + 4ac$
3. $10ac + 25ad + 4bc + 10bd$
4. $x^2 - 19x + 84$
5. $a^2 + 16a + 63$

6. $a^2 - a - 20$
7. $6x^2 + 11x + 3$
8. $25x^2 - 4$
9. $9x^2 - 42x + 49$
10. $25x^2 - 4y^2$

EXERCISE 11l
(p. 204)

1. $15 - 5x$
2. $36x^2 - 24x$
3. $6xy - 15xz$
4. $ac + ad - bc - bd$
5. $x^2 + 3x - 28$

6. $x^2 - 11x + 18$
7. $12x^2 + 11x + 2$
8. $x^2 - 8xy + 16y^2$
9. $4x^2 + 28xz + 49z^2$
10. $1 - 25a^2$

CHAPTER 12   Algebraic Factors

Each type of factor could be introduced as the converse of an expansion from the previous chapter.

EXERCISE 12a We start with common factors which are often forgotten when factorising at a later
(p. 205)   date. Encourage multiplying out to check the results.

1. $4(x+1)$ **4.** $5(a-2b)$ **7.** $4(3a+1)$
2. $3(4x-1)$ **5.** $3(t-3)$ **8.** $2(a+2b)$
3. $2(3a+1)$ **6.** $5(2a-1)$ **9.** $7(2x-1)$

10. $x(x+2)$ **13.** $x(2x+1)$ **16.** $x(x-4)$
11. $x(x-7)$ **14.** $2t(2-t)$ **17.** $b(b+4)$
12. $a(a+6)$ **15.** $x(x+5)$ **18.** $a(4a-1)$

19. $2x(x-3)$ **22.** $4x(3x+4)$ **25.** $2a(a-6)$
20. $2z(z^2+2)$ **23.** $5b(a-2c)$ **26.** $2p(3p+1)$
21. $5a(5a-1)$ **24.** $3y(y+9)$ **27.** $3y(3y-2)$

28. $2(x^2+2x+3)$ **33.** $3(x^2-2x+3)$
29. $5(2a^2-a+4)$ **34.** $4(a^2+2a-1)$
30. $b(a+4c-3d)$ **35.** $x(5y+4z+3)$
31. $4(2x-y+3z)$ **36.** $5b(a+2c+d)$
32. $3a(3b-2c-d)$ **37.** $2y(x-2z+4w)$

38. $x^2(x+1)$ **43.** $a^2(1+a)$
39. $x^2(1-x)$ **44.** $b^2(b-1)$
40. $5a^2(4-a)$ **45.** $2x^2(2x-1)$
41. $4x^2(3x-4)$ **46.** $9a^2(3-2a)$
42. $4x^2(x^2+3)$ **47.** $5x^2(2-3x^2)$

48. $4(3x+2)$ **53.** $x(x-8)$
49. $4x(2x+3)$ **54.** $3(4+3y^2)$
50. $3(3x^2-2x+4)$ **55.** $4x(3y+4z+2)$
51. $5x(x^2-2)$ **56.** $2x(2x^2+3)$
52. $4q(2p+r)$ **57.** $4bc(3a-2d)$

58. $\frac{1}{2}h(a+b)$ **64.** $2g(h_1-h_2)$
59. $m(g-a)$ **65.** $m(\frac{1}{2}v^2-gh)$

60. $\frac{1}{2}m(v^2+u^2)$ **66.** $\frac{\pi r^2}{3}(4r-h)$

61. $P\left(1+\dfrac{RT}{100}\right)$ **67.** $\pi r(3r+2h)$

62. $\pi r(2r+h)$ **68.** $\frac{1}{2}mu(u+1)$
63. $\pi(R^2+r^2)$ **69.** $\frac{1}{4}c(2b-a)$

EXERCISE 12b It is important to point out that it does not matter which bracket is written first,
(p. 208)   i.e. $(x+2)(x+3)$ is identical to $(x+3)(x+2)$.

1. $(x+1)(x+2)$ **6.** $(x+1)(x+7)$
2. $(x+1)(x+5)$ **7.** $(x+6)(x+2)$
3. $(x+3)(x+4)$ **8.** $(x+1)(x+12)$
4. $(x+3)(x+5)$ **9.** $(x+1)(x+15)$
5. $(x+1)(x+20)$ **10.** $(x+2)(x+10)$

11. $(x+4)(x+4)$
12. $(x+3)(x+12)$
13. $(x+1)(x+18)$
14. $(x+2)(x+20)$
15. $(x+1)(x+8)$

16. $(x+3)(x+3)$
17. $(x+2)(x+18)$
18. $(x+3)(x+6)$
19. $(x+5)(x+6)$
20. $(x+4)(x+10)$

EXERCISE 12c
(p. 208)
1. $(x-1)(x-8)$
2. $(x-3)(x-4)$
3. $(x-2)(x-15)$
4. $(x-4)(x-7)$
5. $(x-6)(x-7)$

6. $(x-2)(x-3)$
7. $(x-1)(x-15)$
8. $(x-3)(x-3)$
9. $(x-2)(x-16)$
10. $(x-7)(x-9)$

EXERCISE 12d
(p. 210)
1. $(x+2)(x-3)$
2. $(x+5)(x-4)$
3. $(x-4)(x+3)$
4. $(x-4)(x+7)$
5. $(x+5)(x-3)$

6. $(x-6)(x+4)$
7. $(x-3)(x+9)$
8. $(x-11)(x+2)$
9. $(x-7)(x+5)$
10. $(x-10)(x+2)$

EXERCISE 12e
(p. 211)
To some, the worked example may appear to be too detailed. Most pupils require a definite plan of attack and will find the given method very helpful until they feel confident enough to go straight to the answer.

1. $(x+2)(x+7)$
2. $(x-3)(x-7)$
3. $(x+7)(x-2)$
4. $(x+6)(x-5)$

5. $(x+1)(x+8)$
6. $(x-5)(x-5)$
7. $(x+9)(x-1)$
8. $(x-13)(x-2)$

9. $(x+8)(x-7)$
10. $(x+2)(x+30)$
11. $(x+3)(x-9)$
12. $(x+20)(x-4)$

13. $(x+1)(x+13)$
14. $(x-2)(x+14)$
15. $(x+10)(x-8)$
16. $(x-5)(x-6)$

17. $(x-4)(x+12)$
18. $(x+6)(x+12)$
19. $(x+4)(x+13)$
20. $(x+2)(x-14)$

21. $(x+3)(x+8)$
22. $(x+3)(x-14)$
23. $(x-2)(x-16)$
24. $(x+12)(x-5)$

EXERCISE 12f
(p. 211)
1. $(x+1)(x+8)$
2. $(x-3)(x-3)$
3. $(x+4)(x+7)$
4. $(4-x)(5+x)$

5. $(x+3)(x+3)$
6. $(x-1)(x-8)$
7. $(x+2)(x+15)$
8. $(9+x)(3-x)$

9. $(x+2)(x+11)$
10. $(x-13)(x+2)$
11. $(x-1)(x-7)$
12. $(x-6)(x+7)$

13. $(x-8)(x+3)$
14. $(x-2)(x-7)$
15. $(x+1)(x+27)$
16. $(x-7)(x+9)$

17. $(x+5)^2$
18. $(x-5)^2$
19. $(x+2)^2$
20. $(x-7)^2$

21. $(x+6)^2$
22. $(x-6)^2$
23. $(x-2)^2$
24. $(x+8)^2$

EXERCISE 12g Many pupils need much convincing that $6-5x-x^2$ and x^2+5x-6 do not
(p. 212)   factorise to give the same answers. The problem is not helped later when
$6-5x-x^2 = 0$ becomes $x^2+5x-6 = 0$. Time spent on distinguishing between an
expression and an equation, i.e. on the difference between factorising an expression
and using factors to solve an equation, will be time well spent.

1. $(2+x)(1-x)$ **5.** $(3+x)(2-x)$
2. $(3-x)(2+x)$ **6.** $(2-x)(1+x)$
3. $(1-x)(4+x)$ **7.** $(4+x)(2-x)$
4. $(4-x)(2+x)$ **8.** $(5+x)(1-x)$

9. $(5+x)(2-x)$ **13.** $(6-x)(1+x)$
10. $(6-x)(2+x)$ **14.** $(5+x)(4-x)$
11. $(5-x)(1+x)$ **15.** $(5+x)(3-x)$
12. $(7+x)(2-x)$ **16.** $(4-x)(3+x)$

EXERCISE 12h **1.** $(x+5)(x-5)$ **4.** $(x+1)(x-1)$ **7.** $(x+6)(x-6)$
(p. 213)   **2.** $(x+2)(x-2)$ **5.** $(x+8)(x-8)$ **8.** $(x+9)(x-9)$
                   3. $(x+10)(x-10)$ **6.** $(x+4)(x-4)$ **9.** $(x+7)(x-7)$

10. $(3+x)(3-x)$ **13.** $(a+b)(a-b)$ **16.** $(5+x)(5-x)$
11. $(6+x)(6-x)$ **14.** $(3y+z)(3y-z)$ **17.** $(9+x)(9-x)$
12. $(10+x)(10-x)$ **15.** $(4+x)(4-x)$ **18.** $(x+y)(x-y)$

EXERCISE 12i **1.** $3(x+4)$ **6.** $7(3x-1)$
(p. 214)   **2.** $5x(5x+2)$ **7.** $9x(x-2)$
                   3. $4(3x^2-2)$ **8.** $4(5x+3)$
                   4. $7(2x+3)$ **9.** $2(2x-7)$
                   5. $2(2x^2+1)$ **10.** $4x(2x-1)$

11. $2(x+3)(x+4)$ **16.** $3(x+2)(x+6)$
12. $3(x-1)(x-8)$ **17.** $4(x-3)^2$
13. $7(x+1)^2$ **18.** $5(x+2)(x-3)$
14. $4(x+3)(x-4)$ **19.** $2(x+2)(x-11)$
15. $5(x+1)(x+7)$ **20.** $3(x-5)(x+8)$

EXERCISE 12j **1.** $(2x+1)(x+1)$ **6.** $(3x-2)(x-2)$
(p. 215)   **2.** $(3x-2)(x-1)$ **7.** $(2x+1)(x+4)$
                   3. $(4x+3)(x+1)$ **8.** $(5x-2)(x-3)$
                   4. $(2x-1)(x-3)$ **9.** $(2x+3)(x+4)$
                   5. $(3x+1)(x+4)$ **10.** $(7x-1)(x-4)$

11. $(2x+1)(x-2)$ **16.** $(7x+2)(x-3)$
12. $(3x+4)(x-1)$ **17.** $(6x+5)(x-2)$
13. $(5x+2)(x-3)$ **18.** $(5x-4)(x-3)$
14. $(x+2)(4x-3)$ **19.** $(3x+4)(x-5)$
15. $(3x-2)(x+4)$ **20.** $(4x-3)(x+5)$

EXERCISE 12k   **1.** $(3x+2)(2x+1)$ **6.** $(3x-1)(2x-3)$
(p. 216)   **2.** $(2x+3)(3x+5)$ **7.** $(3x-2)(3x-4)$
3. $(3x+1)(5x+2)$ **8.** $(2x-1)(8x-1)$
4. $(2x+3)(6x+5)$ **9.** $(5x-3)(3x-7)$
5. $(7x+2)(5x+2)$ **10.** $(5x-2)(4x-3)$

11. $(4x+1)(2x-3)$ **16.** $(3a-5)(2a+3)$
12. $(5x-2)(3x+1)$ **17.** $(3t-2)(2t+1)$
13. $(3x+2)(7x-4)$ **18.** $(3b-2)^2$
14. $(10x+3)(8x-3)$ **19.** $(x-2y)(5x+3y)$
15. $(3x+4)(8x-5)$ **20.** $(x-2)(4x-3)$

EXERCISE 12l   **1.** $(2x+5)(2x-5)$ **4.** $(4a+b)(4a-b)$
(p. 217)   **2.** $(3x+2)(3x-2)$ **5.** $(3x+5)(3x-5)$
3. $(6a+1)(6a-1)$ **6.** $(2a+1)(2a-1)$

7. $(4a+3b)(4a-3b)$ **11.** $(2x+7y)(2x-7y)$
8. $(5s+3t)(5s-3t)$ **12.** $(9x+10y)(9x-10y)$
9. $(10x+7y)(10x-7y)$ **13.** $(3a+2b)(3a-2b)$
10. $(3y+4z)(3y-4z)$ **14.** $(8p+9q)(8p-9q)$

15. $3(a+3b)(a-3b)$ **19.** $5(a+2)(a-2)$
16. $2(3t+5s)(3t-5s)$ **20.** $5(3+b)(3-b)$
17. $3(3x+y)(3x-y)$ **21.** $\frac{1}{2}(a+2b)(a-2b)$

18. $5(3x+2)(3x-2)$ **22.** $\left(\frac{a}{2}+\frac{b}{3}\right)\left(\frac{a}{2}-\frac{b}{3}\right)$
or $\frac{1}{36}(3a+2b)(3a-2b)$

23. $\frac{1}{3}(9x+y)(9x-y)$
24. $\left(\frac{x}{4}+\frac{y}{5}\right)\left(\frac{x}{4}-\frac{y}{5}\right)$ or $\frac{1}{400}(5x+4y)(5x-4y)$

EXERCISE 12m   **1.** 7.5   **5.** 31.2   **9.** 1000   **13.** 8
(p. 218)   **2.** 18.5   **6.** 20.4   **10.** 336   **14.** 140
3. 17.7   **7.** 12.9   **11.** 53.2   **15.** 75.8
4. 35.04   **8.** 178.97   **12.** 5.336   **16.** 0.526

EXERCISE 12n This is an important exercise. Forgetting to extract a common factor results in
(p. 218) many expressions being more difficult to factorise than they need be.

1. $5(x+1)(3x+2)$ **6.** $2(x+1)(4x+3)$
2. $2(x-2)(2x+1)$ **7.** $5(x-3)(5x+2)$
3. $3(x+1)(2x+1)$ **8.** $3(x-1)(3x+4)$
4. $3(x-2)(6x+5)$ **9.** $2(x+4)(3x+1)$
5. $2(x+5)(4x-3)$ **10.** $5(x+4)(3x-2)$

11. $2(3x-2)(3x-4)$ **14.** $5(4x-3)(5x-2)$
12. $3(2x-1)(8x-1)$ **15.** $4(2x+1)(3x-2)$
13. $2(2x+1)(3x+2)$ **16.** $7(x+4)(3x-2)$

17. $(4+3x)(1-2x)$
18. $(4-3x)(3+4x)$
19. $(7-x)(3+4x)$
20. $2(2-x)(6-x)$
21. $2(4+x)(2-3x)$

22. $(9-x)(1+x)$
23. $(12+x)(1-x)$
24. $2(2+3x)^2$
25. $5(3-x)^2$
26. $5(2+x)(2+3x)$

EXERCISE 12p
(p. 219)

1. $(x+5)(x+8)$
2. $(3x+1)(2x+1)$
3. $(x+6)(x-6)$
4. Does not factorise

5. $(x-2)(x-6)$
6. $(2x-3)(x+5)$
7. $(x+7)(x-1)$
8. $(5x-2)(x+1)$

9. $(x-3)(x-8)$
10. $(3x+2)(x+3)$
11. $(x+15)(x-1)$
12. $(4x-1)(3x-1)$

13. $(x+2)(x+6)$
14. $(4x+1)(2x-1)$
15. $(x+7)(x-7)$
16. Does not factorise

17. $(3x+2)(2x-5)$
18. $(x+6)(x+7)$
19. $(2x+3y)(2x-3y)$
20. $(5x-4)(3x-2)$

21. $(2x-3)(3x+2)$
22. $(x+13)(x-2)$
23. $2(3x+1)(5x-2)$
24. $(4+x)(7-x)$

25. $(2x-1)(3x+4)$
26. $5(2x+1)(3x+2)$
27. $(x+2)(x+9)$
28. $(x-4)(x-6)$

29. $4(x+2y)(x-2y)$
30. Does not factorise
31. $2(3x+2)(2x-5)$
32. $(x-2)(x+15)$

33. $(2-x)(14+x)$
34. $(a-7)(a-9)$
35. $2(3-2x)(1-2x)$
36. $(1+2x)(1+4x^2)$

37. $(x+17)(x-4)$
38. $(2x-1)(x^3+2)$
39. $3(2x+1)(x-2)$
40. $(p+1)(p^2+1)$

41. $(a+b+c)(a+b-c)$
42. $(29x+1)(4x-1)$
43. $(a+16)(a+7)$
44. $(x^2+y+1)(x^2-y-1)$

45. $(a-8)(3a-7)$
46. $2(x+7)(x-11)$
47. $(2x+y-z)(2x-y+z)$
48. $(ab+18)(ab-19)$

EXERCISE 12q
(p. 220)

1. a) $7a+21$ b) $3x-6y$
2. a) $x^2+14x+40$ b) $6x^2-19x+15$
3. a) $25+10x+x^2$ b) $25-10x+x^2$ c) $25-x^2$
4. a) $10(a+2)$ b) $5p(3p-2)$
5. a) $(a+1)(a^2+1)$ b) $(k+l)(2m-n)$
6. a) $(x-3)(x+9)$ b) $(x-7)(5x-7)$ c) $\left(a+\dfrac{b}{2}\right)\left(a-\dfrac{b}{2}\right)$
7. a) $(5x+2)(2x-3)$ b) $(10a+9b)(10a-9b)$

EXERCISE 12r
(p. 221)

1. a) $5a^2 + 15a$ b) $12x^2 - 8xy$
2. a) $y^2 - 9y + 20$ b) $15x^2 - 14xy - 8y^2$
3. a) $4p^2 + 12pq + 9q^2$ b) $4p^2 - 12pq + 9q^2$ c) $4p^2 - 9q^2$
4. a) $4z^2(2z - 1)$ b) $5y(x - 4z)$
5. a) $(m+1)(2+3n)$ b) $(a+2b)(c-2d)$
6. a) $(x+3)(x-9)$ b) $(4x-1)(x+7)$ c) $(2m+9n)(2m-9n)$
7. a) $3(x-3)(5x-3)$ b) Does not factorise or $5(3 + 5x - 4x^2)$

EXERCISE 12s
(p. 221)

1. a) $4a + 28$ b) $6x^2 - 9xy$
2. a) $x^2 + 12x + 27$ b) $15x^2 - x - 2$
3. a) $25x^2 + 20x + 4$ b) $25x^2 - 20x + 4$ c) $25x^2 - 4$
4. a) $6z(2z - 1)$ b) $4y(2x - 3z)$
5. a) $(z+2)(z^2+1)$ b) $(3a+b)(c+2)$
6. a) $(x-6)(x+4)$ b) $(2a+5)(2a-3)$ c) $\left(3m + \dfrac{n}{3}\right)\left(3m - \dfrac{n}{3}\right)$
7. a) $(5x-3)(3x+2)$ b) $(3+5x)(2-3x)$

CHAPTER 13 Quadratic Equations

This chapter introduces quadratic equations and covers solution by factorisation. Graphical solution, completing the square and using the formula are in Book 4A.

Many of the questions in the first two exercises can be considered orally. They form a useful introduction. It is also worth pointing out that if $A \times B = 0$ then stating that either $A = 0$ or $B = 0$ does not rule out the possibility that both A and B are zero.

EXERCISE 13a
(p. 222)

1. a) 8   b) 0   c) 0   6. a) 33   b) 0   c) 0
2. a) 0   b) 5   c) 0   7. a) -24 b) 0   c) 0
3. a) 0   b) 7   c) 0   8. a) 70   b) 0   c) 0
4. a) 0   b) 0   c) 3   9. a) 0   b) 0   c) 20
5. a) 20   b) 0   c) 6   10. a) -9 b) 0   c) 0

EXERCISE 13b
(p. 223)

1. 0   7. 0   13. a) 0 b) 0
2. 0   8. 2   14. a) 0 b) 0
3. 0   9. 0   15. a) 0 b) 0
4. any value   10. 7   16. a) 0 b) any value
5. 4   11. any value
6. 1   12. 0

17. $a = 0$ or $b = 1$ 22. $a = 0$ or $b = 4$
18. $a = 0$ or $b = 5$ 23. $a = 0$ or $b = 10$
19. $a = 0$ or $b = 2$ 24. $a = 1$ or $b = 0$
20. $a = 3$ or $b = 0$ 25. $a = 7$ or $b = 0$
21. $a = 9$ or $b = 0$ 26. $a = 12$ or $b = 0$

EXERCISE 13c
(p. 225)

1. 0 or 3
2. 0 or 5
3. 0 or 3
4. 0 or -4
5. 0 or -5

6. 0 or 6
7. 0 or 10
8. 0 or 7
9. 0 or -7
10. 0 or -9

11. 1, 2
12. 5 or 9
13. 7 or 10
14. 4 or 7
15. 1 or 6

16. 8 or -11
17. 3 or -5
18. -7 or 2
19. -2 or -3
20. -4 or -9

21. -1 or -8
22. p or q
23. $-a$ or $-b$
24. 4 or -1
25. -9 or 8

26. -6 or -7
27. -10 or -11
28. a or b
29. $-a$ or b
30. c or $-d$

EXERCISE 13d
(p. 226)

1. 1 or $2\frac{1}{2}$
2. 4 or $\frac{2}{3}$
3. $\frac{4}{5}$ or $\frac{3}{4}$
4. 0 or $1\frac{1}{4}$
5. 0 or $\frac{3}{10}$
6. $-\frac{2}{5}$ or 7
7. $-\frac{5}{6}$ or $\frac{2}{3}$
8. $\frac{3}{8}$ or $-2\frac{1}{2}$
9. $1\frac{1}{7}$ or $-3\frac{3}{4}$
10. $-\frac{3}{4}$ or $-1\frac{1}{2}$

11. $2\frac{1}{3}$ or 2
12. $1\frac{2}{3}$ or $\frac{1}{2}$
13. 0 or $\frac{1}{3}$
14. 0 or $\frac{3}{7}$
15. $-1\frac{1}{2}$ or 3
16. $-\frac{3}{4}$ or $2\frac{1}{2}$
17. $-\frac{9}{10}$ or $\frac{4}{5}$
18. $\frac{2}{3}$ or $-2\frac{1}{4}$
19. $2\frac{2}{5}$ or $-3\frac{1}{2}$
20. $-1\frac{3}{5}$ or $-\frac{3}{4}$

EXERCISE 13e
(p. 226)

1. 1 or 2
2. 1 or 7
3. 2 or 3
4. 2 or 5
5. 3 or 4

6. 1 or 5
7. 1 or 11
8. 2 or 4
9. 2 or 6
10. 1 or 12

11. 1 or -7
12. 4 or -2
13. 3 or -4
14. 5 or -3
15. 2 or -9

16. -1 or 13
17. 2 or -3
18. -2 or 6
19. 4 or -5
20. -3 or 8

21. -1 or -2
22. -1 or -7
23. -3 or -5
24. -2 or -6
25. -2 or -9

26. -1 or -6
27. -2 or -5
28. -1 or -13
29. -1 or -15
30. -3 or -6

31. ± 1
32. ± 3
33. ± 4
34. ± 9
35. ± 13

36. ± 2
37. ± 5
38. ± 10
39. ± 12
40. ± 6

EXERCISE 13f
(p. 228)

1. 0 or 2
2. 0 or 10
3. 0 or -8
4. 0 or $\frac{1}{2}$
5. 0 or $\frac{5}{4}$

6. 0 or 5
7. 0 or -3
8. 0 or -1
9. 0 or $\frac{5}{3}$
10. 0 or $\frac{7}{5}$

11. 0 or $-\frac{3}{2}$
12. 0 or $-\frac{5}{8}$
13. 0 or 7
14. 0 or $-\frac{5}{3}$
15. 0 or $\frac{12}{7}$

16. 0 or $-\frac{7}{6}$
17. 0 or $-\frac{7}{12}$
18. 0 or -4
19. 0 or $\frac{2}{7}$
20. 0 or $-\frac{3}{14}$

EXERCISE 13g　**1.** 1 (twice)　**6.** 3 (twice)　**11.** -9 (twice)　**16.** -5 (twice)
(p. 229)　**2.** 5 (twice)　**7.** 4 (twice)　**12.** 7 (twice)　**17.** 6 (twice)
　3. 10 (twice)　**8.** 9 (twice)　**13.** 11 (twice)　**18.** 20 (twice)
　4. -4 (twice)　**9.** -1 (twice)　**14.** -6 (twice)　**19.** 8 (twice)
　5. -3 (twice)　**10.** -10 (twice)　**15.** $\frac{1}{2}$ (twice)　**20.** $-\frac{2}{3}$ (twice)

EXERCISE 13h　**1.** $\frac{1}{2}$ and 2　**6.** $\frac{2}{3}$ and 3　**11.** $-\frac{1}{2}$ and $\frac{2}{3}$　**16.** $\frac{3}{4}$ and $1\frac{1}{2}$
(p. 230)　**2.** $1\frac{1}{2}$ and 4　**7.** $\frac{1}{3}$ and 2　**12.** $\frac{2}{5}$ and $-1\frac{1}{3}$　**17.** $-\frac{5}{6}$ and $2\frac{1}{2}$
　3. $2\frac{1}{2}$ and 4　**8.** $1\frac{1}{2}$ and -4　**13.** $\frac{1}{3}$ and $\frac{1}{4}$　**18.** $-\frac{1}{2}$ and $-1\frac{1}{2}$
　4. -1 and $-\frac{2}{3}$　**9.** $-\frac{2}{3}$ and -3　**14.** $-\frac{1}{3}$ and $2\frac{1}{2}$　**19.** $-\frac{2}{3}$ and $-\frac{3}{4}$
　5. -7 and $2\frac{1}{2}$　**10.** $-\frac{2}{5}$ and -5　**15.** $-\frac{1}{5}$ and $-\frac{3}{4}$　**20.** $3\frac{1}{2}$ and $-\frac{3}{5}$

　21. $\pm\frac{5}{4}$　　　　　　**26.** $\pm\frac{2}{3}$
　22. $\pm\frac{9}{10}$　　　　　**27.** $\pm\frac{5}{9}$
　23. $\pm\frac{5}{2}$　　　　　　**28.** $\pm\frac{2}{5}$
　24. $\pm\frac{4}{3}$　　　　　　**29.** $\pm\frac{5}{6}$
　25. $\pm\frac{12}{5}$　　　　　**30.** $\pm\frac{9}{2}$

EXERCISE 13i　**1.** -5 and 6　　　**5.** 3 and -2
(p. 231)　**2.** -2 and 8　　　**6.** 1 and -7
　3. 3 and -12　　　**7.** $\frac{1}{2}$ and -3
　4. $\frac{2}{3}$ and -2　　　**8.** 3 and $-\frac{3}{5}$

　9. -2 or 4　　　**13.** -2 and 5
　10. -4 and 6　　　**14.** 2 and 4
　11. 5 and 7　　　**15.** $\frac{1}{2}$ and $-\frac{1}{3}$
　12. $-\frac{1}{5}$ or $1\frac{1}{2}$　　**16.** $\frac{1}{3}$ and 4

　17. 2 and 5　　　**21.** 2 and 6
　18. 1 and 7　　　**22.** 4 and 5
　19. 2 and 4　　　**23.** 5 and 7
　20. 3 and 7　　　**24.** 3 and 5

　25. 0 and $\frac{1}{2}$　　　**30.** 0 and 3
　26. 2 and 3　　　**31.** 1 and 2
　27. 2 and 6　　　**32.** -1 and -2
　28. -1 and $-\frac{2}{3}$　　**33.** $\frac{1}{3}$ and 2
　29. $\frac{1}{2}$ and -3　　**34.** $-\frac{1}{5}$ and $1\frac{1}{2}$

EXERCISE 13j　**1.** -4 and 5　　　**5.** -1 and -12
(p. 233)　**2.** 2 (twice)　　　**6.** $\pm\frac{1}{4}$
　3. $\pm\frac{1}{3}$　　　　**7.** 0 and 6
　4. 0 and $-3\frac{1}{2}$　　**8.** -5 and 7

9. 2 and $-3\frac{1}{2}$

10. -3 (twice)

11. 1 and -7

12. $\pm\frac{2}{5}$

13. $\pm 2\frac{1}{2}$

14. -2 and -9

15. $\frac{1}{2}$ and $-\frac{2}{3}$

16. 0 and $2\frac{1}{2}$

17. 2 and $-\frac{1}{3}$

18. $-\frac{1}{2}$ and $-1\frac{1}{3}$

19. 0 and $1\frac{3}{4}$

20. $\frac{1}{3}$ and $\frac{1}{4}$

21. $\frac{1}{3}$ and $-2\frac{1}{2}$

22. $-\frac{1}{3}$ and 2

23. $-\frac{1}{2}$ and $-1\frac{1}{2}$

24. $\pm\frac{1}{2}$

25. 3 and -4

26. 3 and -1

27. $\frac{1}{2}$ and $-\frac{1}{3}$

28. 1 and 4

29. -3 and 8

30. 5 and 7

31. -2 and $\frac{2}{3}$

32. $-\frac{1}{3}$ and 2

33. 5 and -10

34. -11 and 8

35. 5 and -9

36. -2 and 7

37. 7 and -4

38. 5 and -11

39. -4 and -5

40. -4 and -5

41. 0, 1 and 2

42. 0, 3 and -4

43. 0, 2 and $2\frac{1}{2}$

44. 0, 1 and 1

45. 0, $-\frac{1}{2}$ and -4

46. 0, 6 and 7

47. 0, -2 and 5

48. 0, 5 and $-2\frac{1}{3}$

49. 0, $\frac{3}{2}$ and $-\frac{3}{2}$

50. 0, 2 and 4

EXERCISE 13k Above average candidates should find a great deal of satisfaction from this
(p. 235)   exercise.

1. -2 or 8   **2.** -2 or 7   **3.** -7 or 6

4. $x+(x^2-6)=66$; $x=-9$ or 8; 58 marbles

5. $x+x^2=56$; $x=-8$ or 7; Ahmed is 7 and his father is 49

6. $x+(x^2+2)=44$; $x=-7$ or 6; Kathryn is 6 and her mother is 38

7. $x(x+5)=84$; $x=7$ or -12; Peter is 7

8. $x(x-4)=140$; $x=14$ or -10; Ann is 10

9. $x(x+3)=28$; $x=4$ or -7; 4 cm by 7 cm

10. $x(x+5)=66$; $x=-11$ or 6; 6 cm by 11 cm

11. $\frac{1}{2}x\times\frac{1}{2}x=25$; $x=\pm10$; 5 cm

12. a) $A=20x\,\text{m}^2$, $B=x^2\,\text{m}^2$, $C=30x\,\text{m}^2$

b) $x^2+50x=104$; $x=2$ or -52; path is 2 m wide

EXERCISE 13l There are other possible solutions to some of these equations. The given solutions
(p. 238)   are positive numbers but there may be negative ones as well.

Notice that, in some cases, as the value tested goes up the number obtained goes
down and more testing may be needed.

These questions give useful practice in the use of the memory functions in calculators, but note that some working needs to be written down.

Some pupils may find it easier to cope with a more systematic method for finding the numbers to try; in this case, the interval bisection method (i.e. using the value halfway between the two previous values) can be used. This has the advantage that it can be programmed into a computer.

132 Short Programs for the Mathematics Classroom (published by Stanley Thornes (Publishers) Ltd gives examples of programs for finding roots of equations.

1. 1.3 and 1.4	**5.** 1.4 and 1.5
2. 1.3 and 1.4	**6.** 11.2 and 11.3 or 0.7 and 0.8
3. 2.0 and 2.1	**7.** 3.1 and 3.2
4. 2.8 and 2.9	**8.** 2.6 and 2.7

9. a) 3.16 and 3.17   b) 3.2
10. a) 1.62 and 1.63 or 7.37 and 7.38   b) 1.6 or 7.4
11. a) 1.21 and 1.22 or 7.83 and 7.84   b) 1.2 or 7.8
12. a) 4.17 and 4.18   b) 4.2

EXERCISE 13m
(p. 240)

1. a) -10 b) 0   c) 8
2. a) 0 or -7 b) 0 or $\frac{1}{2}$
3. a) 3 and 8   b) 2 and $-\frac{3}{5}$
4. a) 7 and -5 b) 5 and 8
5. a) $\frac{1}{2}$ and $\frac{4}{5}$ b) $\frac{2}{5}$ and $-\frac{1}{3}$ c) $\pm\frac{2}{3}$
6. a) 0 and 2   b) 0 and $\frac{3}{4}$
7. a) 5 and -9 b) 5 and -6
8. 2.5, 2.6

EXERCISE 13n
(p. 240)

1. a) -2 b) 0   c) 12   d) 0
2. a) 0 and 2   b) 0 and $-\frac{3}{7}$
3. a) 2 and -5 b) -2 and $1\frac{1}{3}$ c) $-1\frac{1}{2}$ and $1\frac{1}{2}$
4. a) -3 and 2   b) -5 and -6
5. a) $\frac{1}{5}$ and $-\frac{3}{4}$ b) $-\frac{2}{5}$ and $-2\frac{1}{3}$
6. a) 0 and $-\frac{2}{3}$ b) 0 and $-\frac{3}{7}$
7. a) -4 and 8   b) -2 and 4
8. 19.6, 19.7 or 0.3, 0.4

EXERCISE 13p
(p.240)

1. a) -11 b) 0   c) 0
2. a) 0, -7 b) 0, $\frac{3}{4}$
3. a) $-4, 5$ b) $1\frac{3}{4}, -3$ c) $\frac{3}{5}, -\frac{3}{5}$
4. a) 5, -3 b) $-4, -8$
5. a) $-\frac{1}{5}, -\frac{3}{4}$ b) $-\frac{2}{7}, \frac{1}{4}$
6. a) 0, $-1\frac{1}{3}$ b) 0, $-1\frac{2}{3}$
7. a) $-5, 2$ b) $-10, 3$
8. 1.3, 1.4

CHAPTER 14   Graphs

This chapter concentrates on the practical aspect of graphs—drawing acceptable curves, making up tables from formulae and reading values from the graph.

It is worth starting by showing some examples of graphs which give a misleading impression. For example, ask pupils what these graphs show:

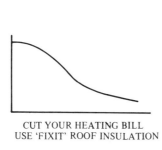

CUT YOUR HEATING BILL
USE 'FIXIT' ROOF INSULATION

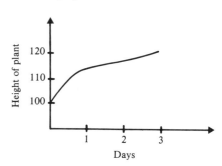

Ask the pupils to bring in some examples of graphs from magazines etc., for discussion.

We have used a dot within a circle ⊙ to mark points on a graph. Some may prefer to use a cross, i.e. × or +.

In early graphical work some pupils may fail to draw a satisfactory curve first time. It would be wiser to get them to re-draw it on a fresh sheet, using the benefit of the first unsatisfactory attempt, than to rush on to a new question. While a few pupils will be most unlikely to draw an acceptable curve, most pupils' graphical work can be improved significantly by careful attention to the section headed "Points to remember when drawing graphs of curves".

EXERCISE 14a   **1.** a) $200t$ b) 3.16 cm   **4.** a) 3 cm   b) 67 cm^2
(p. 243)   **2.** a) £168.9   b) 7.27 years   **5.** a) 16.5 cm   b) 2.21
                            3. a) 3.6   b) 2.3

EXERCISE 14b   **1.** a) 59.5 m   b) 4.47 s   **4.** 2.65, 5.29
(p. 247)   **2.** a) 4.8   b) 7.5   **5.** a) 3.33   b) −1.43
                            3. a) 1.67   b) 1.09

EXERCISE 14c   For the most able it is worth pointing out that they are using their graphs to solve
(p. 249)   quadratic equations. A computer can be used to solve some of these equations
                            more accurately; it may also be used to investigate quadratic graphs generally.

1. The graph passes through the origin O, which also gives the lowest value for y.
2. a) 1.73 or −1.73   b) No
3. a) 2 and −2   b) 1 and −1, Yes

4. They all have the same shape.
They all have the same shape but cross the y-axis at different points.

5. a) When $x = 0$ and $x = 3$ b) -0.79 and 3.79

6. a) When $x = 0$ and 1.5 b) $-1\frac{1}{8}$ when $x = \frac{3}{4}$

7. a) -2 when $x = -1$ b) 10.5 c) 0 and -2

8. a) -4 when $x = 1$
b) (i) -1.24 and 3.24 (ii) -2.46 and 4.46

9. a) 6.25 when $x = 0.5$
b) (i) -2.37 and 3.37 (ii) -1 and 2

CHAPTER 15   Polygons

This chapter starts with the sum of the exterior angles and then deduces the sum of the interior angles. Some teachers may prefer to do this the other way round and here are two methods:

1. Building polygons up from triangles:

Number of triangles = number of sides -2
So the sum of the interior angles of an n-sided polygon
= the sum of the interior angles of $(n-2)$ triangles
= $(n-2)\,180°$

2. Taking a point inside a polygon:

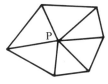

An n-sided polygon gives n triangles
So the sum of the interior angles of the polygon
= the sum of the interior angles of n triangles $-$ angle sum at P
= $(180n - 360)°$

**EXERCISE 15a
(p. 254)**

1. No, angles not equal

2. Yes

3. No, sides not equal

4. No, $\begin{cases} \text{sides not equal} \\ \text{angles not equal} \end{cases}$

5. No, $\begin{cases} \text{sides not equal} \\ \text{angles not equal} \end{cases}$

6. No, $\begin{cases} \text{sides not equal} \\ \text{angles not equal} \end{cases}$

7. Yes

8. No, not bounded by straight lines

EXERCISE 15b **1.** 180°
(p. 256) **2.** 360°
3. a) $p = 100°$, $r = 135°$, $x = 55°$, $q = 125°$ b) 360°
4. a) $w = 120°$, $x = 60°$, $y = 120°$, $z = 60°$ b) 360°
5. a) 180°   b) 540°   c) 180°   d) 360°
6. 360°
7. a) equilateral   b) 60°   c) 120°   d) 60°   e) 360°

EXERCISE 15c To demonstrate the sum of the exterior angles, a ruler can be placed along one side
(p. 258) and then slid and turned until it is back to its original position.

1. 60°	**6.** 90°	**11.** $x = 50°$
2. 90°	**7.** 95°	**12.** $x = 30°$
3. 50°	**8.** 55°	**13.** $x = 24°$
4. 50°	**9.** 30°	**14.** a) 5 b) 8
5. 60°	**10.** 125°	

EXERCISE 15d **1.** 36°   **4.** 60°   **7.** 40°
(p. 261) **2.** 45°   **5.** 24°   **8.** 22.5°
3. 30°   **6.** 20°   **9.** 18°

EXERCISE 15e **1.** 720°   **4.** 360°   **7.** 2880°
(p. 262) **2.** 540°   **5.** 900°   **8.** 1260°
3. 1440°   **6.** 1800°   **9.** 2340°

EXERCISE 15f **1.** a) 3240°   b) 2520°   c) 1620°
(p. 263) **2.** 80°   **4.** 110°   **6.** 85°
3. 120°   **5.** 105°   **7.** 110°

8. 108°   **10.** 135°   **12.** 150°
9. 120°   **11.** 144°   **13.** 162°

14. a) 18   b) 24   **15.** a) 12   b) 20
16. a) yes, 12   b) yes, 9   c) no   d) yes, 6   e) no   f) yes, 4
17. a) yes, 4   b) yes, 6   c) no   d) yes, 72   e) yes, 36   f) yes, 8

EXERCISE 15g In Numbers 15–20 the most able should give reasoned answers. In many cases the
(p. 265) teacher may decide that appeal to symmetry is acceptable.

1. 54°	**6.** 50°	**11.** 72°	**15.** a) 36° b) 36°
2. 45°	**7.** 80°	**12.** 45°	**16.** a) 128.6° b) 25.7°
3. 150°	**8.** 135°	**13.** 60°	**17.** 77.1°
4. 72°	**9.** 100°	**14.** 36°	**18.** a) 22.5° b) 22.5°
5. 60°	**10.** 60°		**19.** 22.5°
			20. 45°

EXERCISE 15h Number 6 can be used to take the idea of tessellations further, i.e. some shapes built
(p. 271) up from squares and equilateral triangles will tessellate. For example:

After tessellations with shapes that *do* work, pupils can try these two shapes (which
do not tessellate)

and then investigate some shapes of their own.

1. a) The interior angles (135°) do not divide exactly into 360°
   b) A square
2. a) No   b) A regular ten-sided polygon
4. Square, equilateral triangle

CHAPTER 16   Probability

The use of "dice" as the singular is controversial. We have kept to "dice" rather
than "die" because it is common usage.

EXERCISE 16a The work in this exercise revises the work in Book 2A on the probability of a single
(p. 273) event.

1. a) $\frac{4}{9}$ b) $\frac{7}{9}$ c) 1   d) 0
2. a) $\frac{1}{13}$ b) $\frac{1}{4}$ c) $\frac{9}{13}$
3. a) $\frac{31}{90}$ b) $\frac{1}{10}$
4. a) $\frac{21}{26}$ b) $\frac{4}{13}$ c) $\frac{7}{26}$
5. a) 1   b) $\frac{1}{5}$
6. a) $\frac{4}{9}$ b) $\frac{5}{9}$
7. 0.53
8. a) $\frac{4}{9}$ b) $\frac{5}{9}$
9. $\frac{1}{3}$
10. $\frac{151}{153}$
11. $\frac{4}{7}$

EXERCISE 16b This section introduces the idea of addition of probabilities for mutually exclusive
(p. 277) events, but the words "mutually exclusive" are not used. Plenty of discussion is
needed, with other examples, to illustrate the idea of separate events, i.e. situations
when either A or B can occur, but not both. The scores on a dice give a simple
illustration, e.g. *P*(either a 2 or a 3) is $P(2)+P(3)$, but *P*(a 2 or a prime) is *not*
$P(2)+P(\text{prime})$.

1. a) $\frac{1}{6}$ b) $\frac{1}{6}$ c) $\frac{1}{3}$
2. a) $\frac{5}{9}$ b) $\frac{4}{9}$
3. a) $\frac{3}{10}$ b) $\frac{7}{10}$
4.

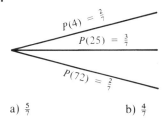

   a) $\frac{5}{7}$ b) $\frac{4}{7}$

6.

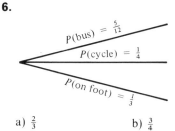

   a) $\frac{2}{3}$ b) $\frac{3}{4}$

5.

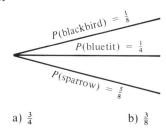

   a) $\frac{3}{4}$ b) $\frac{3}{8}$

7. 2
8. 80
9. 3
10. 50

EXERCISE 16c Revises the work in Book 2A on possibility spaces.
(p. 281)
1. a) $\frac{5}{36}$ b) $\frac{1}{6}$ c) 0
2. a) $\frac{1}{4}$ b) $\frac{3}{4}$ c) $\frac{1}{2}$
3. a) $\frac{7}{12}$ b) $\frac{2}{3}$ c) $\frac{13}{36}$
4. a) $\frac{1}{4}$ b) $\frac{1}{4}$ c) $\frac{1}{9}$
5. a) $\frac{1}{2}$ b) $\frac{1}{4}$ c) $\frac{1}{4}$
6. a) $\frac{1}{4}$ b) $\frac{3}{4}$
7. a) $\frac{7}{12}$

EXERCISE 16d All questions on probability trees use independent events. Dependent events are
(p. 283) introduced in Book 4A.

1. a) $\frac{2}{5}$

b)

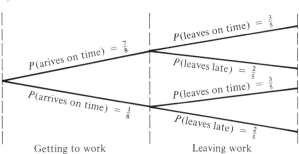

c) $\frac{7}{20}$ d) $\frac{3}{40}$

2. a) $\frac{3}{4}$

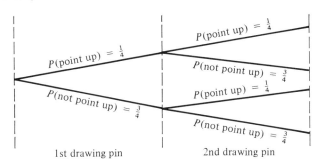

b) $\frac{1}{16}$ c) $\frac{9}{16}$

3.

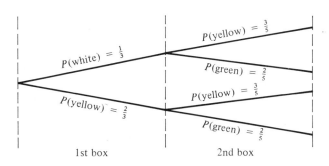

a) $\frac{2}{5}$ b) $\frac{2}{15}$

4. (i) a) $\frac{1}{6}$ b) $\frac{5}{6}$

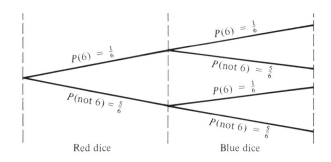

Red dice   Blue dice

(ii) a) $\frac{1}{36}$ b) $\frac{5}{36}$ c) $\frac{5}{36}$ d) $\frac{5}{18}$

EXERCISE 16e   1.
(p. 285)

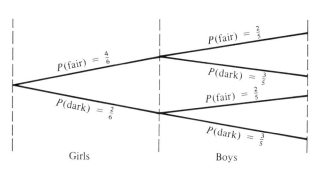

Girls   Boys

$\frac{8}{15}$

2.

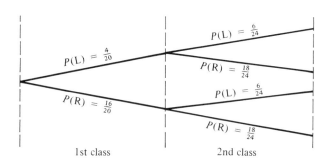

1st class   2nd class

$\frac{7}{20}$

3.

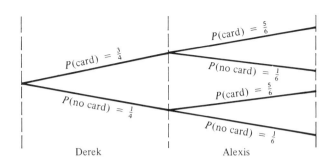

a) $\frac{5}{8}$ b) $\frac{1}{3}$ c) $\frac{1}{24}$ d) 1

4.

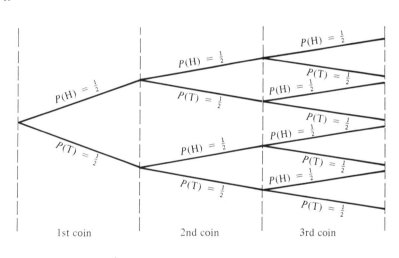

a) $\frac{1}{8}$ b) $\frac{1}{8}$ c) $\frac{3}{8}$

EXERCISE 16f **1.** a) $\frac{4}{11}$ b) $\frac{4}{11}$
(p. 286) **2.** a) 0 b) 1
3. a) $\frac{1}{4}$ b) $\frac{1}{8}$ c) $\frac{1}{8}$
4. a) $\frac{3}{32}$ b) $\frac{7}{16}$

5. b) and d) $\frac{4}{15}$

a)

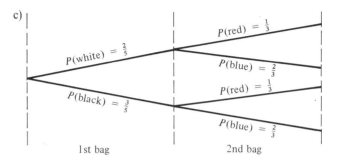

c)

CHAPTER 17   Ratio and Proportion

The first part of this chapter is revision of the work in Book 2A, although problems with mixed units are dealt with more thoroughly here.

EXERCISE 17a   **1.** $2:3$ **4.** $2:3$ **7.** $4:9$
(p. 288)   **2.** $1:2:3$ **5.** $18:8:9$ **8.** $3:5:4$
                    3. $7:5$ **6.** $2:3:1$ **9.** $2:3:1$

10. $6:11$ **12.** $31:4$
11. $15:4$ **13.** $5:16$

14. $1.5:1$ **17.** $2.73:1$ **20.** $1.33:1$
15. $2.4:1$ **18.** $0.6:1$ **21.** $0.75:1$
16. $0.857:1$ **19.** $2.63:1$ **22.** $1.43:1$

EXERCISE 17b   **1.** $9:2$ **3.** $17:60$ **5.** $9:20$
(p. 289)   **2.** $2:5$ **4.** $2:125$ **6.** $50:3$

7. $20:19$ **8.** $36:35$ **9.** $27:25$ **10.** $9:10$

11. $25:24$ **12.** a) $3:2$ b) $2:3$ c) $3:5$

13. a) $2:3$ b) $9:5$ c) $21:23$ d) $6:5$

14. $18:25$ **15.** a) $1:1$ b) $1:2$ c) $1:8$ d) $1:1$ e) $1:3$ f) $1:8$

16. a) $1:9$ b) $1:4$ c) $4:9$

EXERCISE 17c
(p. 291)

1. $1\frac{1}{9}$ or 1.11 **3.** $7\frac{1}{2}$ or 7.5 **5.** 24
2. $\frac{3}{7}$ or 0.429 **4.** $1\frac{3}{7}$ or 1.43 **6.** $22\frac{1}{2}$

7. $9\frac{1}{3}$ or 9.33 **9.** $1\frac{1}{5}$ or 1.2 **11.** $3\frac{1}{3}$ or 3.33
8. $2\frac{8}{11}$ or 2.73 **10.** $7\frac{1}{5}$ or 7.2 **12.** $8\frac{4}{7}$ or 8.57

13. 12 grandsons; $3:7$ **15.** 10.1 cm
14. 152   **16.** 264

EXERCISE 17d
(p. 293)

1. £20, £25   **5.** 18 boys, 14 girls
2. 54 m, 42 m   **6.** $60°$, $50°$, $70°$
3. 0.625 kg, 1.25 kg, 3.125 kg   **7.** 9, 12, 9
4. $\frac{1}{2}$ hr, $2\frac{1}{2}$ hrs, 4 hrs   **8.** 66 hits, 24 misses

EXERCISE 17e
(p. 294)

1. $9:7$ **6.** $5:3$
2. 30 m, 42 m   **7.** $500:53$
3. $5\frac{1}{4}$ **8.** $4:3$
4. $2\frac{2}{9}$ or 2.22 **9.** $3:4$
5. 27.5 cm   **10.** $\frac{2}{3}$

Proportion: There are many different methods for dealing with problems on proportion but some of them are seen as black magic by the children.
Whichever method is used it should be used exclusively to avoid confusion.

Science and other subjects make great demands on the children's mathematical ability and particularly so in proportion problems, so it is as well for them to be familiar with the type of problem liable to crop up. They should also be prepared to use decimals as well as whole numbers.

The unitary method is based on the simplest idea but is not always the easiest to carry out and some people find the ratio method requires less work.

The third method is what some people call the "common sense" method, that is, to use a multiplying factor as in the following example:

At a steady speed a car uses 4 litres of petrol to travel 75 km. How much is needed for 60 km?

Amount needed $= 4 \times \frac{60}{75}$ km $\Big($ we multiply by $\frac{60}{75}$ because *less* petrol is required to travel 60 km than 75 km $\Big)$.

However, deciding on the multiplying factor can cause worry, as "common sense" does not always come into play. (This method used to be called "the rule of three".)

EXERCISE 17f
(p. 295)
1. a) £2.70   b) £10.80
2. a) 6 units   b) $\frac{3}{4}$ unit
3. a) 72 km   b) 118.8 km
4. a) 35 rows   b) 42 rows
5. a) £1.65   b) £7.92

EXERCISE 17g
(p. 295)
1. £1.20
2. 15.5 km
3. $4\frac{1}{3}$ or 4.33 km
4. £3.65
5. £9.80
6. £4.20
7. £8.30
8. 1.5 p
9. 1.5 m
10. 5.5 m^2

EXERCISE 17h
(p. 297)
1. 3.2 litres
2. 3 hours
3. $12\frac{1}{2}$ units
4. 3.6 hours
5. a) £45   b) 350 miles
6. £144
7. 700
8. £3.96
9. 66 rows
10. 20.25 cm

11. £336
12. 480
13. 65.6 km
14. a) 2.25×10^7 b) 8.1×10^6 c) 1.35×10^5
15. 15 V
16. 24.7 joules
17. 82.6 p, 83 p
18. £14.05

Inverse Proportion: If a multiplying factor is used for direct proportion then it can also be used for inverse proportion, using common sense to decide which way up the factor should be. This method can only be used for numerical problems.

The unitary method is simpler than the ratio method for inverse proportion.

EXERCISE 17i
(p. 300)
1. $5\frac{1}{2}$ hours
2. 12
3. 203
4. 8 days
5. 25 cm
6. 20
7. 16 cm
8. 44
9. 48

EXERCISE 17j
(p. 302)
1. a) 10 350   b) 5.22
2. £145.35
3. $3\frac{1}{2}$ hours
4. No answer
5. 4.46 cm
6. 49
7. 24
8. 34
9. 1.44 m
10. 6 weeks
11. No answer
12. 1.5 amps

EXERCISE 17k
(p. 303)
1. 3 : 1
2. $3\frac{3}{5}$ or 3.6
3. 8 m, 16 m, 32 m
4. 114 km (3 s.f.)
5. 6 hours 40 mins
6. 6 : 2 : 1
7. 9
8. $\frac{6}{5}$: 1 or 1.2 : 1

EXERCISE 17l
(p. 303)
1. 4 : 3
2. 12, 8, 20
3. $6\frac{3}{5}$ or 6.6
4. 8 : 7
5. 0.6 : 1
6. £7.50
7. 1 : 3
8. £37.50

CHAPTER 18 Trigonometry

Exercises 18a to 18i repeat the work in Book 2A although there is a fuller introduction in Book 2A with work on drawing and measuring and on similar triangles.

Use of calculator: When two sides of a right-angled triangle are given, pupils can find an angle without a break to write down the value of the trig ratio. There are two reasons for discouraging this; firstly, many children cannot see their way through the complete calculation without the break; secondly, even if the calculation is done in one, the intermediate steps should be written down in case a mistake is made at the next stage. Some children make the jump from, for example, $\frac{x}{2} = \tan 20°$ to the value of x. This should be strictly discouraged as examining boards expect an explicit expression for x before the calculation, i.e. $x = 2 \tan 20°$. When the intermediate step is written down, it is not sensible to write down all the figures from the display; the first four significant figures will give answers correct to three significant figures.

EXERCISE 18a
(p. 305)

7. $\frac{5}{12}$, 0.4167
8. $\frac{8}{15}$, 0.5333
9. $\frac{3}{4}$, 0.75
10. $\frac{3}{4}$, 0.75
11. $\frac{12}{5}$, 2.4
12. $\frac{35}{12}$, 2.917

EXERCISE 18b
(p. 307)

1. 1.8807
2. 0.2493
3. 0.5890
4. 0.3019
5. 0.0805
6. 3.0777
7. 4.8716
8. 1
9. 0.5774
10. 1.1184
11. 0.0524
12. 0.5635

13. 10.1°
14. 19.6°
15. 55.0°
16. 23.4°
17. 53.7°
18. 32.3°
19. 42.7°
20. 38.7°
21. 17.8°
22. 69.6°
23. 42.7°
24. 0.1°

EXERCISE 18c
(p. 308)

1. 32.0°
2. 63.4°
3. 23.2°
4. 35.8°
5. 51.3°
6. 60.9°

7. 31.0°
8. 51.3°
9. 48.4°
10. 47.7°
11. 34.2°

EXERCISE 18d
(p. 309)

Some teachers may prefer to write $\tan 32° = \frac{x}{4}$.

1. 2.44 cm
2. 5.40 cm
3. 2.56 cm
4. 6.72 cm
5. 17.0 cm
6. 81.8 cm
7. 5.62 cm
8. 22.2 cm
9. 2.82 cm
10. 7.54 cm
11. 3.60 cm
12. 11.4 cm

13. 2.42 cm
14. 1.76 cm
15. 46.6 cm
16. 10.4 cm
17. 4.69 cm
18. 366 cm
19. 0.976 cm
20. 69.5 cm

EXERCISE 18e
(p. 312)

1. 0.8862	4. 0.1564	7. 0.8625	10. 0.4664
2. 0.9397	5. 0.2622	8. 0.5	11. 0.2723
3. 0.2470	6. 0.6088	9. 0.9903	12. 0.9988

13. 15.7°	16. 65.4°	19. 37.9°
14. 26.2°	17. 41.8°	20. 46.7°
15. 31.6°	18. 21.8°	21. 7.1°

EXERCISE 18f
(p. 313)

1. 30°	4. 44.4°	7. 44.4°	10. 19.5°
2. 17.5°	5. 14.5°	8. 41.8°	11. 4.38 cm
3. 48.6°	6. 62.7°	9. 23.6°	12. 10.6 cm

13. 1.46 cm	15. 11.7 cm	17. 6.31 cm	19. 3.34 cm
14. 4.57 cm	16. 23.2 cm	18. 21.9 m	20. 45.7 cm

EXERCISE 18g
(p. 315)

1. 0.8480	4. 0.6717	7. 0.6143
2. 0.7455	5. 0.5	8. 0.6561
3. 0.1392	6. 0.9632	9. 0.3040

10. 69.7°	13. 69.6°	16. 30.1°
11. 20.6°	14. 51.1°	17. 89.2°
12. 44.0°	15. 71.6°	18. 85.8°

EXERCISE 18h
(p. 316)

1. 34.9°	4. 48.2°	7. 50.2°	10. 25.8°
2. 36.9°	5. 48.2°	8. 66.4°	11. 34.0°
3. 45.6°	6. 53.1°	9. 81.4°	

12. 3.50 cm	15. 11.6 cm	18. 17.1 cm	20. 4.12 cm
13. 26.9 m	16. 38.2 cm	19. 2.23 cm	21. 13.5 cm
14. 1.96 cm	17. 2.90 cm		

EXERCISE 18i
(p. 319)

1. 40.0°	6. 33.7°	11. 68.5°	15. 39.3°
2. 33.6°	7. 39.8°	12. 14.5°	16. 55.6°
3. 51.3°	8. 33.7°	13. 56.9°	17. 42.1°
4. 42.8°	9. 37.7°	14. 37.8°	18. 66.2°
5. 35.5°	10. 53.1°		

19. 6.69 cm	23. 4.48 cm	27. 13.7 cm	32. 7.45 cm
20. 19.3 cm	24. 80.5 cm	28. 3.08 cm	33. 14.5 cm
21. 8.03 cm	25. 6.04 cm	29. 113 cm	34. 21.4 cm
22. 4.86 cm	26. 3.50 cm	30. 2.59 cm	35. 74.5 cm
		31. 9.99 cm	36. 60.6 cm

EXERCISE 18j
(p. 322)

1. 4.13 cm	4. 4.67 cm	7. 4.40 cm	9. 33.1 cm
2. 8.72 cm	5. 14.9 cm	8. 14.9 cm	10. 42.6 cm
3. 23.3 cm	6. 17.0 cm		

EXERCISE 18k Angles of elevation and depression will need revision. There are more problems
(p. 324) using trigonometry in Chapters 19 and 20.

1. 8.99 m
2. 47.7 m
3. 143 m
4. 39.8°
5. 61.6°
6. 56.3°
7. 48.2°

8. 11.3°
9. a) 5.30 cm   b) 6.25 cm
10. a) 5.20 cm   b) 15.6 cm²
11. 4.66 m
12. a) $A\hat{O}B = 72°$, $O\hat{A}B = 54°$
    b) 6.88 cm
    c) 34.4 cm², 172 cm²

CHAPTER 19   Pythagoras' Theorem

EXERCISE 19a
(p. 326)

1. 38.44
2. 187.7
3. 58 560
4. 7 728 000

5. 0.5041
6. 0.003 481
7. 0.000 002 89
8. 97 340

9. 9.734
10. 0.000 973 4
11. 84.64
12. 8464

13. 27 140 000
14. 2714
15. 0.2714
16. 0.002 714

17. 3.142
18. 4.461
19. 11.14
20. 311.1

21. 0.2195
22. 0.069 43
23. 9.798
24. 17.92

25. 1.619
26. 0.2490
27. 0.027 93
28. 0.7071

29. 0.6790
30. 2.147
31. 21.47
32. 0.021 47

EXERCISE 19b
(p. 328)

1. 10.3 m
2. 15.3 m
3. 3.22 m

4. 136 cm
5. 23.0 cm
6. 102 cm

7. 12.6 cm
8. 7.97 cm
9. 2.31 cm

10. 5.31 cm
11. 0.8 cm
12. 73.3 cm

13. 50 cm
14. 26 cm
15. 4.4 cm

16. 100 cm
17. 2.4 cm
18. 20 cm

EXERCISE 19c This revises work done in Book 2A. Remind pupils again to use at least four
(p. 331) significant figures if possible, when writing down the intermediate steps.

1. Yes
2. Yes

3. No
4. No

5. Yes
6. No

Some pupils may be interested in the following variation of Pythagoras' Theorem.

If any mathematically similar figures are drawn on the three sides of a right-angled
triangle, a result similar to Pythagoras' Theorem applies, e.g.

a) if three equilateral triangles are
   drawn on the sides as shown then

   area A = area B + area C

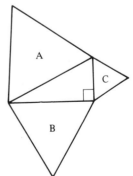

b) if three semicircles
   are drawn on the sides then

   area 1 = area 2 + area 3

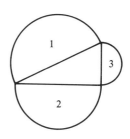

EXERCISE 19d   **1.** 18.9 cm   **5.** 20.5 cm   **9.** 3.58 cm   **12.** 3.13 cm
(p. 332)   **2.** 6.52 cm   **6.** 4.16 cm   **10.** 64.5 cm   **13.** 26.2 cm
                     3. 2.02 cm   **7.** 0.05 cm   **11.** Yes   **14.** Yes, $\hat{\text{M}} = 90°$
                     4. 0.0265 cm   **8.** 13.0 cm

EXERCISE 19e   **1.** 8.94 units   **3.** 5.52 m, 35.4°   **5.** 21.2 cm
(p. 333)   **2.** 38.8 n.m.   **4.** 0.589 m

                     6. a) 39.4 cm   b) 47.9°
                     7. a) 2.4 cm   b) 4.64 cm   No. $AC^2 \neq AB^2 + BC^2$
                     8. c) AC = 7.07 cm, AD = 8.66 cm, AE = 10 cm
                     9. Use 7 cm and 4 cm or 8 cm and 1 cm. $\sqrt{65} = 8.06$

EXERCISE 19f   Many pupils do not find it easy to draw three dimensional figures on paper or to
(p. 335)   extract other figures from them. A lot of practice in drawing cuboids and then
                     triangles from the cuboid is recommended. The use of squared paper is a help and
                     so are wire models.

                     1. a) EA = FB = GC = HD; AB = EF = HG = DC; BC = FG = EH = AD;
                             24 right angles
                         b) EB = 5 cm, $E\hat{B}A = 36.9°$ c) FC = 12.4 cm, $F\hat{C}B = 14.0°$
                     2. a) AC = 12.6 cm   b) $E\hat{A}C = 90°$, EC = 13 cm, $E\hat{C}A = 13.3°$
                     3. a) FC = 8.25 cm   b) AF = 5.39 cm, $F\hat{A}B = 21.8°$
                         c) EG = 9.43 cm, 32.0°

EXERCISE 19g   **1.** a) 14.4 cm   b) 15.3 cm   c) 19.1°
(p. 336)   **2.** a) 3.61 cm   b) 33.7°   c) 6.71 cm
                     3. a) 10 cm   b) 15.6 cm   c) 39.8°
                     4. a) 14.9 cm   b) 19.1 cm   c) 19.1 cm   d) 47.5°   e) 47.7°
                     5. 24.7 cm
                     6. a) 15 cm   b) 16.6 cm   c) 25.0°
                     7. a) 7.07 cm   b) 7.07 cm   c) 600 cm²
                     8. a) 33.7°   b) 56.3°   c) 31.4°
                     9. a) 7.07 cm   b) 336 cm²

EXERCISE 19h   **1.** a) AB = DC = FE, BC = AD, EC = FD, 14 right angles
(p. 338)   b) $E\hat{B}C = 33.7°$, BE = 7.21 cm
                         c) AC = 11.7 cm, $C\hat{A}B = 31.0°$, Yes
                         d) AE = 12.3 cm, AE = FB

2. a) 3.00 cm   b) 7.42 cm   c) 10.9 cm   d) 15.4°
3. a) 27.5 m   b) 48.5m   c) 29.2 m   d) 49.5 m
   e) 11.6 m   f) 53.8°
4. a) 24.4°   b) 13.9°
5. a) 2.62 cm   b) 3.98 cm   c) 5.76 cm

EXERCISE 19i   **1.** a) $A\hat{B}C$, $B\hat{C}D$, $C\hat{D}A$, $D\hat{A}B$, $A\hat{F}B$, $B\hat{F}C$, $C\hat{F}D$, $D\hat{F}A$, $B\hat{F}E$, $C\hat{F}E$, $D\hat{F}E$, $A\hat{F}E$.
(p. 339)   (12). $AE = BE = CE = DE$
        b) $AC = 2.83$ cm, $AF = 1.41$ cm
        c) $EF = 5.83$ cm, $E\hat{C}F = 76.4°$
    2. a) $AC = 5.66$ cm, $AF = 2.83$ cm
        b) $AE = 5.74$ cm, $E\hat{A}F = 60.5°$
        c) $EG = 5.39$ cm, $E\hat{G}F = 68.2°$
    3. a) $E\hat{B}A = 36.9°$, $E\hat{D}A = 45°$
        b) 5 cm   c) 5.83 cm
    4. a) $PR = 8.54$ cm   b) $PY = 4.27$ cm
        c) 54.5°   d) 7.37 cm

EXERCISE 19j   **1.** a) 7.28 m   b) 31.2°   c) 23.3 m, 17.3°
(p. 340)   **2.** a) $AC = CD' = AD' = 5.66$ cm. Equilateral triangle
        b) Rectangle; $AC' = A'C = BD' = DB' = 6.93$ cm
    3. a) $BD = 8.49$ m, $BE = 4.24$ m
        b) $EF = 4.24$ m. Height = 8.49 m
        c) 45°
    4. a) 7.07 cm   c) 4.85 cm
    5. a) $BD = 8.94$ cm   b) $D\hat{B}A = 26.6°$
        c) 11.3 cm
        d) $DC = BD = 8.94$ cm   e) $D\hat{C}A = D\hat{B}A = 26.6°$

CHAPTER 20   Three Figure Bearings

This chapter gives an opportunity to practice angle calculations and the use of Pythagoras' Theorem and Trigonometry.

EXERCISE 20a Revises three figure bearings.
(p. 342)

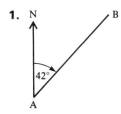

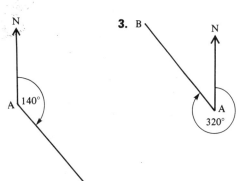

4.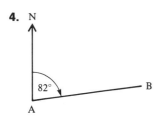

6.

8.

5.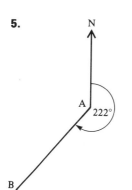

7.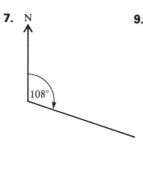

9.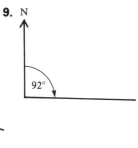

10. 062°   **12.** 328°   **14.** 249°   **16.** 154°
11. 098°   **13.** 262°   **15.** 254°   **17.** 050°

18.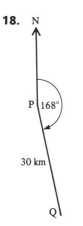

19.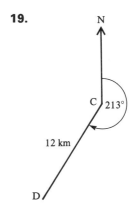

20.

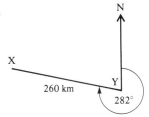

21.

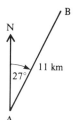

22.

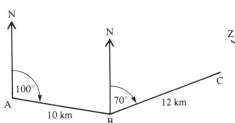

23.

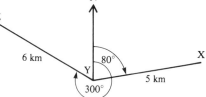

24.

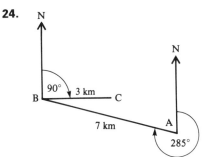

25.

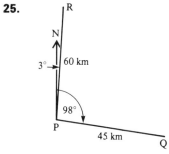

26.

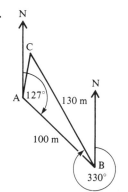

27.

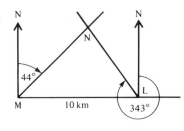

EXERCISE 20b   **1.** 240°   **3.** 342°   **5.** 172°
(p. 346)   **2.** 112°   **4.** 032°   **6.** 305°

EXERCISE 20c
(p. 347)

1. 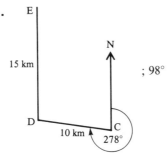 ; 98°

5. 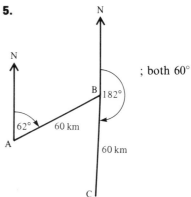 ; both 60°

2. 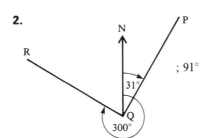 ; 91°

6. 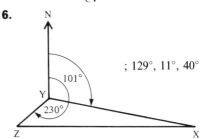 ; 129°, 11°, 40°

3. 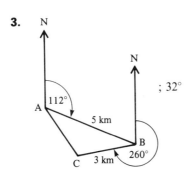 ; 32°

7. 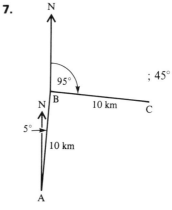 ; 45°

4. 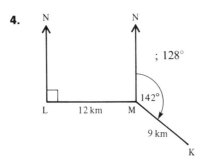 ; 128°

8. 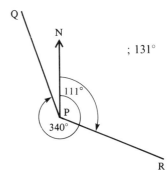 ; 131°

EXERCISE 20d **1.**
(p. 348)

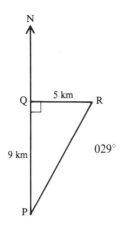

029°

5.

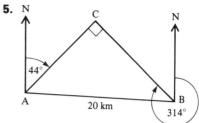

a) 46°, 44°, 90°   b) 14.4 km

2.

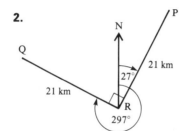

90°, 29.7 km

6.

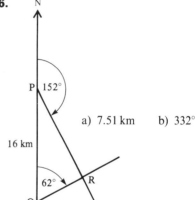

a) 7.51 km   b) 332°

3.

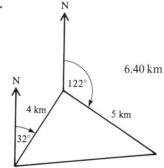

7.

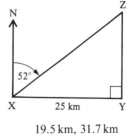

19.5 km, 31.7 km

4. a) 5.81 km   b) 144°

8.

a) 54.5°   b) 186.5°   c) 007°

CHAPTER 21   Inequalities and Regions

This chapter can be used in conjunction with the chapter on straight lines because boundary lines have to be drawn or equations of lines have to be found. Squared paper is satisfactory for the graphical work and a scale of 1 cm to 1 unit is recommended. We have concentrated on shading the regions *not* required, i.e. the required region is unshaded, because this gives a neater solution which can be done on one diagram. However, because examination questions on this topic vary and sometimes they ask for the required region to be shaded, we have given some examples of this type. Exercise 21f shows how to deal with the more complicated cases when the required region has to be shaded. This is a good opportunity to emphasise the importance of reading questions carefully and giving the answer that is asked for. The last section (Exercises 21h to 21j) is a preparation for linear programming. We give an example of a linear programming problem here, which can be used with the pupils to show them the practical applications of the work in this chapter; the topic will be developed more fully in Book 5A.

Linear programming problem

I need to buy at least 6 cakes and I must not spend more than 90 p. Cherry slices cost 10 p each and cup cakes cost 12 p each. Cherry slices are more popular than cup cakes so I must buy at least twice as many cherry slices as cup cakes.

I buy x cherry slices and y cup cakes. I cannot buy a negative number of cakes so $x \geq 0$ and $y \geq 0$.

I buy at least 6 cakes so $x+y \geq 6$:

x cherry slices cost 10 p each so their total cost is $10x$ p.

y cup cakes cost 12 p each so their total cost is $12y$ p.

I must not spend more than 90 p so $10x + 12y \leq 90$.

I buy at least twice as many cherry slices as cup cakes so $x \geq 2y$.

Draw the diagram in the usual way.

If I mark the points with integer co-ordinates we can see what choice I have about how many cakes to buy.

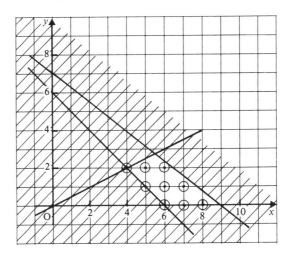

EXERCISE 21a Numbers 27 to 30 give the required region shaded.
(p. 352)

1.
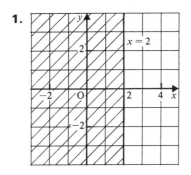

3.
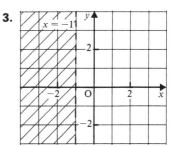

2.
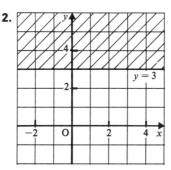

4.
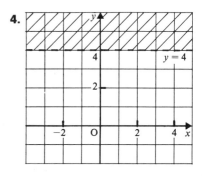

5.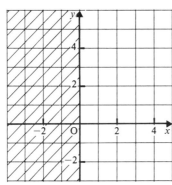

6.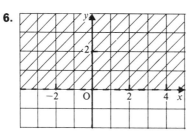

7.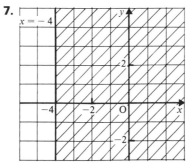

8.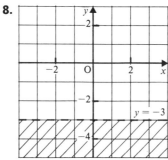

9.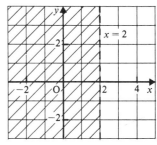

10.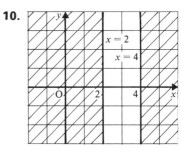

11.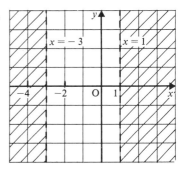

12.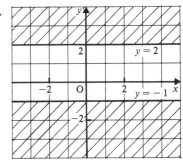

13.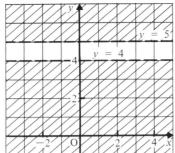

16.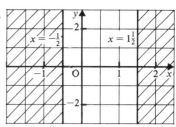

14.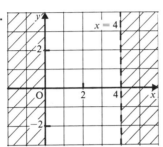

17.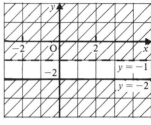

15.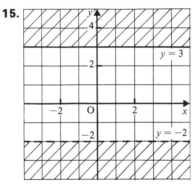

18.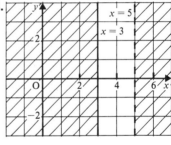

19. 10: No   11: No   12: No

20. $x \leqslant 2$

21. $y < 3$

22. $x < -1$

23. $-2 \leqslant y \leqslant 2$

24. $-1 \leqslant x < 2$

25. $-\frac{1}{2} < y < 2\frac{1}{2}$

26. 20: Yes   21: Yes   22: No   23: Yes   24: No   25: No

27. $-3 \leqslant x \leqslant 1$

28. $-4 < y < -1$

29. $2 \leqslant y < 3$

30. $3 \leqslant x \leqslant 6$

31. 27: Yes   28: No   29: Yes   32: No

EXERCISE 21b
(p. 356)

1.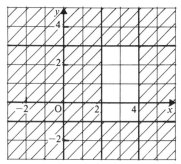

5.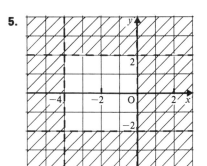

2.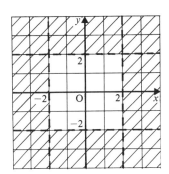

6.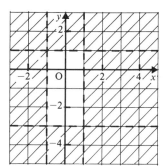

3.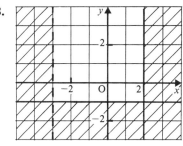

7.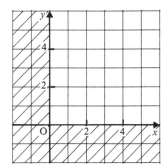

4.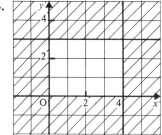

8.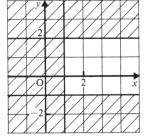

9. $-2 \leqslant x \leqslant 3, \ -1 \leqslant y \leqslant 2$

10. $-2 < x \leqslant 2, \ -2 \leqslant y \leqslant 1$

11. 9: Yes   10: Yes

12. $-2 \leqslant x \leqslant 1, y \geqslant -1$ **15.** $1 < x < 3, 1 < y < 3$

13. $x < 0, y > 0$ **16.** $x \geqslant -2, y \leqslant -1$

14. $-2 < x < 2, -2 < y < 2$ **17.** $x < 1, -2 < y < 2$

18. 16: Yes   17: No

EXERCISE 21c Some children find it easier to decide if a point is in the required region when the
(p. 359) equation of the boundary line is in the form $ax + by = c$ so these come first in the
exercise. The second section deals with boundary lines whose equations are of the
form $y = ax + b$.

1.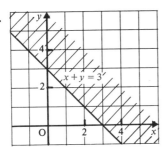

4.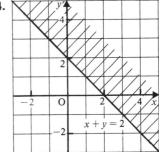

2.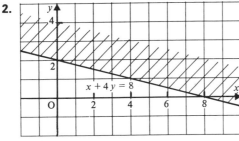

5.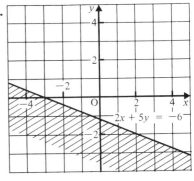

3.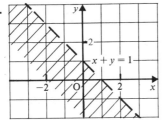

6.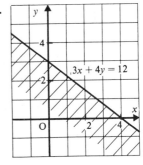

7.

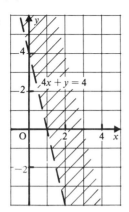

$4x + y = 4$

10.

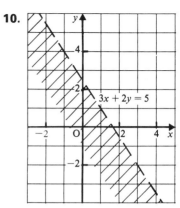

$3x + 2y = 5$

8.

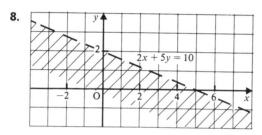

$2x + 5y = 10$

11.

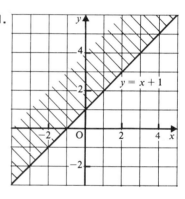

$y = x + 1$

9.

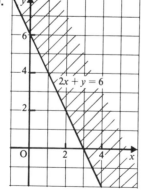

$2x + y = 6$

12.

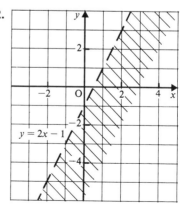

$y = 2x - 1$

13.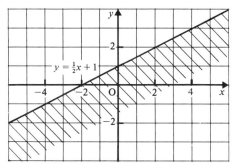

16.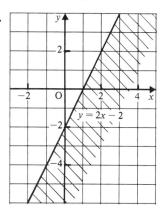

14.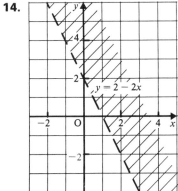

17.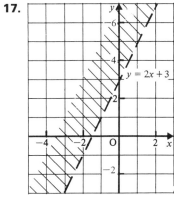

15.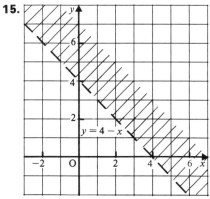

18.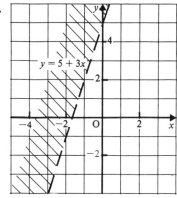

19.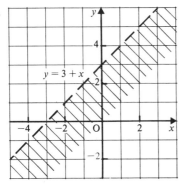

21.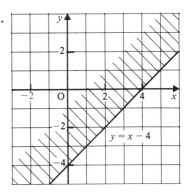

20.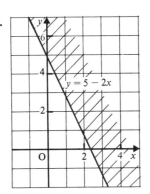

22.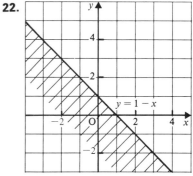

EXERCISE 21d   **1.** $x + y \leqslant 3$
(p. 361)   **2.** $2x + y \geqslant 2$
                      3. $x + 2y < 2$

4. $x + y < 2$
5. $3x - y \leqslant 3$
6. $2y - 3x \leqslant 6$

7. $y \leqslant x + 1$
8. $y > -2x - 4$
9. $y \geqslant \frac{1}{2}x + 2$
10. $y > -x + 2$ or $x + y > 2$

11. $y \geqslant 2x - 2$
12. $y < -\frac{1}{2}x + 2$ or $x + 2y < 4$
13. $y \leqslant 2x + 2$

EXERCISE 21e Suitable ranges are $-6 \leqslant x \leqslant 6$ and $-6 \leqslant y \leqslant 6$.
(p. 364)

1.
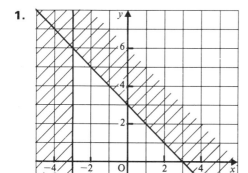

4.
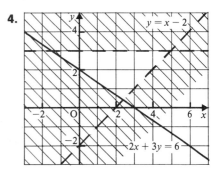

2.
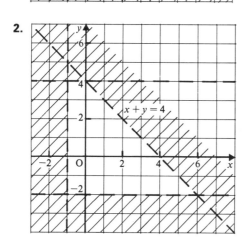

5.
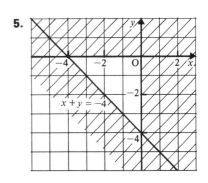

3.
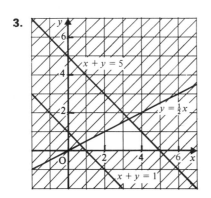

6.
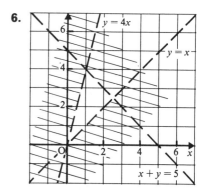

7.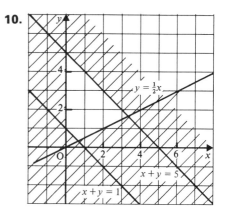

10.

8.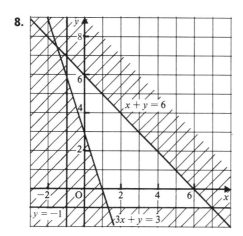

11.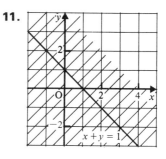

9.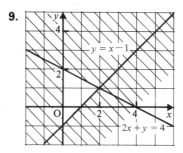

12. It does not exist

13. a) Region consists of 1 point $(1, 2)$
  b) Region does not exist

EXERCISE 21f
(p. 366)

1.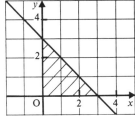

4.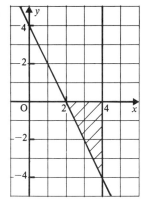

2.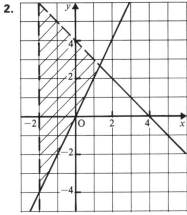

5.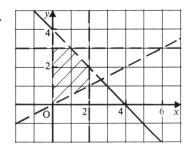

3.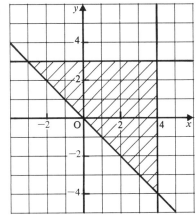

6.

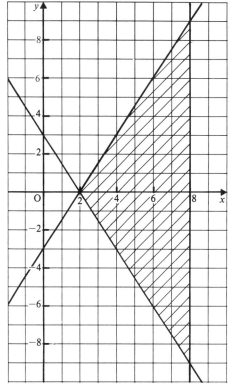

8.

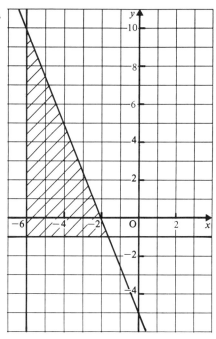

7.

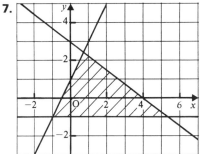

9.

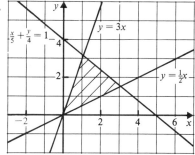

10.

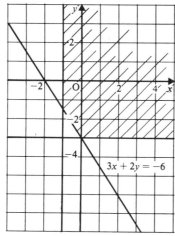

$3x + 2y = -6$

EXERCISE 21g **1.** $x \geqslant -1$, $y \geqslant -2$, $x+y \leqslant 3$
(p. 368) **2.** $y \geqslant 0$, $2y \leqslant x+2$, $x+y \leqslant 4$
3. $y \leqslant x-3$, $2y \geqslant x-6$
4. $x \leqslant 1$, $y \leqslant x+1$, $3x+y > -3$
5. $y > -1$, $x+y < 3$, $y \leqslant 2x+2$
6. $y \geqslant 0$, $x \geqslant -1$, $y \leqslant x+2$
7. $y < 3x+3$, $y > 3x-3$
8. $y \leqslant \frac{1}{3}x+1$, $y \geqslant -\frac{1}{3}x-1$, $y \geqslant \frac{5}{3}x-7$
9. a) $x+y \leqslant 3$, $4y \geqslant x$, $y \leqslant x+3$
b) $4y \leqslant x$, $x+y \geqslant 3$
c) $y \leqslant x+3$, $x+y \geqslant 3$, $4y \geqslant x$
d) $4y \leqslant x$, $x+y \leqslant 3$, $y \leqslant x+3$
e) $y \geqslant x+3$, $x+y \geqslant 3$
f) $x+y \leqslant 3$, $4y \geqslant x$, $y \geqslant x+3$
10. a) $x+y \leqslant 1$, $y \leqslant 2x+4$
b) $y \leqslant 2$, $x+y \geqslant 1$
c) $y \geqslant 2$, $y \leqslant 2x+4$
d) $y \geqslant 2x+4$, $x+y \geqslant 1$
e) $x+y \leqslant 1$, $y \geqslant 2x+4$
f) $y \leqslant 2$, $y \leqslant 2x+4$
11. a) C b) A c) B

EXERCISE 21h **1.** $(2,2)$, $(-2,4)$, $(-2,-2)$ **3.** $(1,-2)$, $(1,1.5)$, $(6,-2)$
(p. 371) **2.** $(2,3)$, $(-1,0)$, $(0,-2)$ **4.** $(1,1)$, $(7,3)$, $(4,6)$, $(-4,6)$

5.

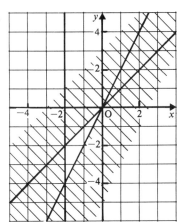

$(-2, -4)$, $(-2, -2)$, $(0, 0)$

6.

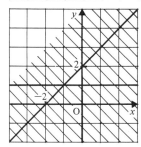

$(0, 1)$, $(0, 2)$ and $(-1, 1)$

7. 1. 19 points $(-2, -2)$, $(-2, -1)$, $(-2, 0)$, $(-2, 1)$, $(-2, 2)$, $(-2, 3)$,
$(-2, 4)$, $(-1, -1)$, $(-1, 0)$, $(-1, 1)$, $(-1, 2)$, $(-1, 3)$, $(0, 0)$,
$(0, 1)$, $(0, 2)$, $(0, 3)$, $(1, 1)$, $(1, 2)$, $(2, 2)$

    2.   4 points $(0, 0)$, $(1, 1)$, $(0, -1)$, $(0, -2)$

    3. 20 points $(-6, -2)$, $(-5, -2)$, $(-4, -2)$, $(-4, -1)$, $(-3, -2)$, $(-3, -1)$,
$(-2, -2)$, $(-2, -1)$, $(-2, 0)$, $(-1, -2)$, $(-1, -1)$, $(-1, 0)$,
$(0, -2)$, $(0, -1)$, $(0, 0)$, $(0, 1)$, $(1, -2)$, $(1, -1)$, $(1, 0)$, $(1, 1)$

8. 13 points $(-1, 0)$, $(-1, 1)$, $(-1, 2)$, $(-1, 3)$, $(0, -1)$, $(0, 0)$, $(0, 1)$, $(0, 2)$,
$(0, 3)$, $(1, 0)$, $(1, 1)$, $(1, 2)$, $(2, 1)$

9.   3 points $(1, 1)$, $(2, 1)$, $(1, 2)$

10. 10 points $(2, -1)$, $(2, 0)$, $(2, 1)$, $(2, 2)$, $(3, -1)$, $(3, 0)$, $(3, 1)$, $(4, -1)$, $(4, 0)$, $(5, -1)$

EXERCISE 21i **1.** 5, 2, −4   **3.** 11, −14, 0
(p. 374)   **2.** 4, −3, 7   **4.** 5, 22; At $(2, -8)$

              5. 10, −1; At $(3, 8)$

              6. a) $(-2, -1)$, $(3, -1)$, $(3, 3)$, $(0, 3)$ b) $(3, 3)$ c) $(-2, -1)$

                  d) 20   e) No

              7. a) $(6, 0)$, $(0, 3)$, $(-2, -3)$ b) $(6, 0)$

              8. a) $(4, 1)$, $(-2, 2)$, $(-2, 5)$ b) (i) $(4, 1)$ (ii) $(-2, 5)$

                  c) $(-2, 3)$, $(-2, 4)$, $(-1, 2)$, $(-1, 3)$, $(-1, 4)$, $(0, 2)$, $(0, 3)$, $(1, 2)$, $(1, 3)$,
$(2, 2)$; 10 points

                  d) No

              9. b) $(5, -3)$, $(-2, 4)$, $(-2, -3)$ c) 33 points

                  d) greatest at $(5, -3)$, least at $(-2, 4)$

EXERCISE 21j **1.** $(1, 2)$ **4.** $(0, 4)$, $(1, 2)$, $(2, 0)$, $(3, -2)$
(p. 377)   **2.** $(2, -2)$ **5.** $(0, 3)$
             3. $(2, -1)$ **6.** $(0, 3)$; No

CHAPTER 22   Coordinates in Three Dimensions

We strongly recommend that in this exercise liberal use is made of squared paper, models and a set of identical cubes.

EXERCISE 22a
(p. 381)   **1.** a) $(3, 2, 1)$ b) $(3, 3, 3)$ c) $(5, 2, 1)$ d) $(2, 4, 2)$ e) $(2, -1, 2)$ f) $(-3, 2, 3)$

2. a)

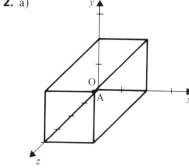

c)

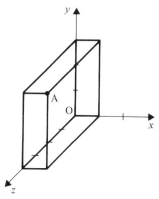

b)

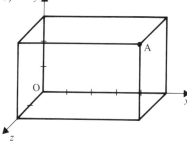

d)

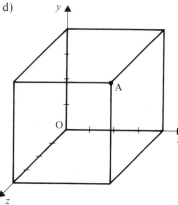

e)

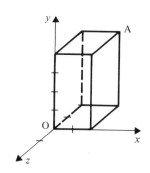

3. P(0, 2, 2), Q(1, 2, 2), R(1, 3, 1), S(2, 2, 1), T(3, 1, 2), U(3, 1, 0), V(0, 0, 2), W(1, 3, 0)

4. A(3, 3, 2), B(2, 3, 1), C(−1, 3, 3), D(−1, 3, 0), E(3, 2, 3), F(3, 0, 1)

5. a) O(0, 0, 0), A(0, 3, 3), B(3, 3, 3), C(3, 3, 0), D(0, 3, 0), E(0, 0, 3), F(3, 0, 3), G(3, 0, 0)
   b) (i) $(3, 3, 1\frac{1}{2})$ (ii) $(3, 1\frac{1}{2}, 3)$ (iii) $(1\frac{1}{2}, 3, 0)$ (iv) $(0, 3, 1\frac{1}{2})$
   c) (i) $(1\frac{1}{2}, 1\frac{1}{2}, 3)$ (ii) $(3, 1\frac{1}{2}, 1\frac{1}{2})$ (iii) $(1\frac{1}{2}, 3, 1\frac{1}{2})$

6. a) (2, 0, 3) b) (2, 6, 3)   c) (2, 0, 0)

7. O(0, 0, 0), A(4, 0, 0), D(4, 0, 4), C(0, 0, 4), G(0, 4, 4), E(4, 4, 4), B(0, 4, 0), F(4, 4, 0)

8. O(0, 0, 0), A(4, 0, 0), B(0, 6, 0), C(0, 0, 2), G(0, 6, 2), F(4, 6, 0), D(4, 0, 2)

9. a) A(−5, 4, 0), C(3, 4, 2), D(−5, 4, 2), E(−5, 0, 0), F(3, 0, 0) G(3, 0, 2), H(−5, 0, 2)
   b) (i) (−1, 4, 0),   (ii) (−1, 4, 2)

10. 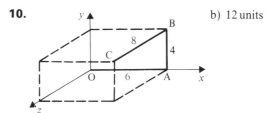   b) 12 units

11. 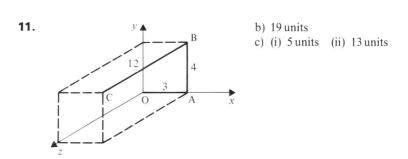   b) 19 units
                                 c) (i) 5 units   (ii) 13 units

12. 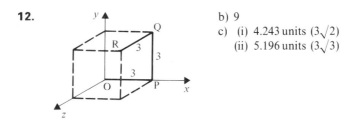   b) 9
                                 c) (i) 4.243 units $(3\sqrt{2})$
                                    (ii) 5.196 units $(3\sqrt{3})$

13.

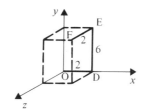

b) 10

c) (i) 6.325 units $(2\sqrt{10})$

(ii) 6.633 units $(2\sqrt{11})$

14. a) $(0, -3, 3)$ b) $(3, -3, 3)$ c) $(3, 0, 3)$

CHAPTER 23

The work in this chapter provides a lot of extra practice in factorising quadratic expressions. It does not include those fractions which, after addition, can be further simplified by factorising the numerator and cancelling common factors. These will be covered in Book 4A.

EXERCISE 23a
(p. 386)

1. $\dfrac{x}{4}$

2. $\dfrac{a}{2}$

3. $\dfrac{p}{q}$

4. $\dfrac{a}{b}$

5. $\dfrac{x}{y}$

6. $\dfrac{1}{2a}$

7. $\dfrac{a}{2c}$

8. $\dfrac{2}{q}$

9. $\dfrac{pq}{2}$

10. $\dfrac{a}{c}$

11. $\dfrac{a}{2}$

12. $\dfrac{z}{2}$

13. $\dfrac{b}{d}$

14. $\dfrac{1}{3x}$

15. $\dfrac{q}{2}$

16. $\dfrac{2}{3y}$

17. $\dfrac{m}{k}$

18. $\dfrac{s}{4t}$

EXERCISE 23b
(p. 388)

1. $\dfrac{1}{x}$

2. $\dfrac{t}{s-t}$

3. Not possible

4. Not possible

5. $\dfrac{x}{2(x-y)}$

6. $\dfrac{(a+b)}{2ab}$

7. $p-q$

8. $\dfrac{1}{(4-a)}$

9. Not possible

10. $\dfrac{1}{v}$

11. $\dfrac{y}{x+y}$

12. $\tfrac{1}{2}$

13. $\dfrac{2a}{3(a-b)}$

14. $\dfrac{2(x-y)}{3xy}$

15. Not possible

16. $u-v$

17. Not possible

18. $\dfrac{1}{(s-6)}$

EXERCISE 23c **1.** $\dfrac{2a}{4a-b}$
(p. 389)

2. $\dfrac{2q}{p-q}$

3. $\dfrac{1}{a}$

4. $\dfrac{3}{5}$

5. $\dfrac{2-x}{3y}$

6. $\dfrac{a}{3-b}$

7. $\dfrac{1}{3a}$

8. s

9. $\dfrac{3}{a}$

10. $\dfrac{2x}{3x-y}$

11. $\dfrac{3a}{a+b}$

12. $\dfrac{p+q}{5}$

13. $\dfrac{1}{3}$

14. $\dfrac{3+a}{4b}$

15. $\dfrac{2-y}{x}$

16. $\dfrac{1}{3y}$

17. a

18. $\dfrac{p}{2}$

19. $\dfrac{1}{a-2}$

20. $\dfrac{1}{x-4}$

21. $\dfrac{1}{y+2}$

22. $\dfrac{2}{a+3}$

23. $\dfrac{3}{x+3}$

24. $\dfrac{9}{y+2}$

25. $\dfrac{y}{x-2}$

26. $\dfrac{q}{p+2}$

27. $\dfrac{t}{s-7}$

28. $\dfrac{1}{p+3}$

29. $\dfrac{1}{x+6}$

30. $\dfrac{2}{x-4}$

31. $\dfrac{3}{x-4}$

32. $\dfrac{v}{u+6}$

33. $\dfrac{y}{x-2}$

EXERCISE 23d **1.** $\dfrac{x+3}{2x-1}$
(p. 391)

2. $\dfrac{4}{x+2}$

3. $\dfrac{2x-1}{x-2}$

4. $\dfrac{1}{2-x}$

5. $\dfrac{a+b}{a-b}$

6. $\dfrac{a+b}{2a+b}$

7. $\dfrac{x-y}{3x-2y}$

8. $\dfrac{2-x}{y}$

9. $-a$

10. $\dfrac{y+3}{2y+1}$

11. $\dfrac{x-3y}{x}$

12. $\dfrac{4x+1}{4x}$

13. $\dfrac{2x-3}{x-5}$

14. $\dfrac{-1}{1+a}$

15. $a+b$

16. $\dfrac{-(x+5)}{(x+1)}$

17. $\dfrac{2(2x-1)}{x-3}$

18. $\dfrac{x-2y}{y}$

19. $\dfrac{1-x}{3(x+2)}$

20. $\dfrac{1+y}{x+y}$

EXERCISE 23e
(p. 392)

1. $\dfrac{ac}{bd}$

2. $\dfrac{ad}{bc}$

3. $\dfrac{5(x-y)}{2x}$

4. $\dfrac{x(x-y)}{10}$

5. $\dfrac{a}{bc}$

6. $\dfrac{ac}{b}$

7. $\dfrac{3(a-b)}{4(a+b)}$

8. $\dfrac{(x-2)(x+3)}{3}$

9. $\dfrac{x-2}{3(x+3)}$

10. $\dfrac{pr}{q}$

11. $\dfrac{6b}{a}$

12. $\dfrac{q}{2p}$

13. $\dfrac{12y}{x}$

14. $\dfrac{2b^2}{5}$

15. $\dfrac{pq}{6}$

16. $\dfrac{x}{2y}$

17. $\dfrac{1}{2b}$

18. $\dfrac{2}{3p}$

19. $\dfrac{a}{4b}$

20. $\dfrac{a^3}{b^3}$

21. $\dfrac{1}{4(b-2)}$

22. $2(x-2)$

23. $2(a+3)$

24. 6

25. $x-3$

26. $x-3$

27. $\dfrac{1}{x-2}$

28. $\dfrac{2}{x+4}$

29. $\dfrac{3(x-2)}{5(x+6)}$

30. $\dfrac{2(2x-3)}{9}$

31. $\dfrac{3}{3x+2}$

32. $\dfrac{2x-3}{2}$

33. $\dfrac{2x-1}{6x+1}$

34. a

35. $\dfrac{-c(a+b)}{b}$

36. $(x-4)(x-2)$

EXERCISE 23f
(p. 395)

A reminder, with explanation, is needed yet again that, for example, a cannot be cancelled in $\dfrac{3}{ab}+\dfrac{a}{2}$. Numerical examples show this clearly,

e.g. $\dfrac{1}{2}+\dfrac{4}{5}$ is *not* $1\dfrac{2}{5}$ $\left(\dfrac{1}{\cancel{2}_1}+\dfrac{\cancel{4}^2}{5}\neq 1\dfrac{2}{5}\,!\right)$.

1. pq
2. rst
3. 30
4. abc
5. $wxyz$

6. ad
7. uvw
8. 168
9. pqr

10. xy
11. $2x^2$
12. $3pq$
13. $2x^2y$
14. abc

15. st
16. $3p^2$
17. $5ab$
18. $3pq^2$

19. $6x$
20. $8x$

21. $18a$
22. 60

23. a^2b
24. $30x$

25. $12x$
26. $15y$
27. $12x$

EXERCISE 23g
(p. 396)

1. $\dfrac{x+y}{xy}$

2. $\dfrac{3q+2p}{pq}$

3. $\dfrac{2t-s}{st}$

4. $\dfrac{6b+a}{2ab}$

5. $\dfrac{5y-6x}{15xy}$

6. $\dfrac{2b+5a}{2ab}$

7. $\dfrac{2y-3x}{xy}$

8. $\dfrac{4q+6p}{3pq}$

9. $\dfrac{3y-2x}{xy}$

10. $\dfrac{20b+21a}{28ab}$

11. $\dfrac{5}{6x}$

12. $-\dfrac{1}{35x}$

13. $\dfrac{5}{4y}$

14. $\dfrac{1}{8p}$

15. $\dfrac{13}{8a}$

16. $\dfrac{4}{21x}$

17. $\dfrac{6}{35x}$

18. $\dfrac{1}{3y}$

19. $\dfrac{3a+2b}{4ab}$

20. $\dfrac{ab-2a^2}{2b^2}$

21. $\dfrac{3y-4}{xy}$

22. $\dfrac{4-3p}{2p^2}$

23. $\dfrac{9a^2+2b^2}{12ab}$

24. $\dfrac{10q-3p}{4pq}$

25. $\dfrac{2s+ts^2}{2t^2}$

26. $\dfrac{15b+4}{6ab}$

27. $\dfrac{3+2x}{3x^2}$

28. $\dfrac{4y^2-9x^2}{6xy}$

29. $\dfrac{5y+4x}{8xy}$

30. $\dfrac{pq+3p^2}{3q^2}$

31. $\dfrac{10y-3}{14xy}$

32. $\dfrac{18b-3a}{2a^2b}$

33. $\dfrac{3x^2-3y^2}{2xy}$

34. $\dfrac{14q-15p}{18pq}$

35. $\dfrac{5a^2+4ab}{5b^2}$

36. $\dfrac{21+8p}{15pq}$

EXERCISE 23h
(p. 398)

1. $\dfrac{9x+3}{20}$

2. $\dfrac{5-x}{12}$

3. $\dfrac{13x+1}{15}$

4. $\dfrac{4x+13}{12}$

5. $\dfrac{1-2x}{35}$

6. $\dfrac{7x+3}{10}$

7. $\dfrac{3x+9}{35}$

8. $\dfrac{5x-3}{42}$

9. $\dfrac{5-22x}{21}$

10. $\dfrac{7x+9}{12}$

11. $\dfrac{22-13x}{6}$

12. $\dfrac{11-7x}{12}$

13. $\dfrac{20-17x}{24}$

14. $\dfrac{22-7x}{20}$

15. $\dfrac{10-5x}{6}$

16. $\dfrac{31x-6}{24}$

17. $\dfrac{11-7x}{10}$

18. $\dfrac{2-11x}{18}$

19. $\dfrac{26x+34}{15}$

20. $\dfrac{17x-1}{12}$

21. $\dfrac{5x-19}{21}$

22. $\dfrac{42x-49}{10}$

23. $\dfrac{27x+3}{14}$

24. $\dfrac{19x-73}{9}$

25. $\dfrac{26x-18}{15}$

26. $\dfrac{-17x+104}{30}$

27. $\dfrac{3a+6}{a(a+3)}$

28. $\dfrac{6x+4}{x(x+2)}$

29. $\dfrac{7x-4}{2x(x-4)}$

30. $\dfrac{2x-3}{4x(2x+1)}$

31. $\dfrac{5a+12}{a(a+4)}$

32. $\dfrac{7x-4}{x(x-1)}$

33. $\dfrac{11x+1}{3x(2x+1)}$

34. $\dfrac{21x-6}{5x(2x+3)}$

EXERCISE 23i
(p. 401)

1. $\dfrac{2c-ab}{ac}$

2. $\dfrac{qr^2}{p}$

3. $\dfrac{7x-14}{12}$

4. $\dfrac{a}{a-b}$

5. $\dfrac{1}{12x}$

6. $\dfrac{1}{x+2}$

7. $\dfrac{-p}{p+q}$

8. $\dfrac{12-2x}{3x^2}$

9. $\dfrac{1-2x}{x(x+1)}$

10. $\dfrac{ab}{c}$

11. $\dfrac{8}{15}$

12. $\dfrac{23}{20x}$

13. $\dfrac{3}{10x^2}$

14. $\dfrac{4x+7}{10}$

15. $\dfrac{(x+4)(2x-1)}{50}$

16. $\dfrac{25}{12x}$

17. $\dfrac{25}{24x^2}$

18. $\dfrac{3}{2}$

19. $\dfrac{19x-1}{3x(x-1)}$

20. $\dfrac{2}{x(x-1)}$

21. $\dfrac{-a-3}{2a(a-1)}$

22. $\dfrac{3}{a(a-1)}$

23. $\dfrac{3}{y}$

24. -1

EXERCISE 23j Remind pupils of the difference between an equation and an expression.
(p. 402)

1. 8	**6.** 5	**11.** 2	**17.** $-2\frac{1}{2}$
2. -5	**7.** $9\frac{3}{5}$	**12.** -18	**18.** -17
3. 6	**8.** $5\frac{1}{4}$	**13.** 3	**19.** 2
4. $1\frac{1}{3}$	**9.** -1	**14.** -1	**20.** 4
5. 10	**10.** $8\frac{3}{4}$	**15.** 21	**21.** 1
		16. $\frac{4}{9}$	**22.** $-2\frac{1}{19}$

23. $-2, -1$	**26.** $-3, -3$	**29.** 1, 1	**31.** $2, -\frac{2}{3}$
24. 3, 2	**27.** 1, -4	**30.** $\frac{2}{3}, 1$	**32.** $-2, -1$
25. $-2, -2$	**28.** $-3, -3$		

33. $4\frac{1}{2}$	**36.** $-2\frac{4}{5}$	**39.** 0, 4	**41.** $\frac{1}{2}, -\frac{1}{2}$
34. $\frac{2}{5}$	**37.** -40	**40.** 3	**42.** 3
35. 2, 1	**38.** $\frac{2}{5}$		

EXERCISE 23k
(p. 405)

1. a) $\dfrac{b}{2}$ b) a c) $a-b$

2. a) $\dfrac{4}{3x}$ b) $\dfrac{1}{3x^2}$ c) 3

3. a) -13 b) 3, -1

4. a) $\dfrac{5x-7}{6}$ b) $1\frac{7}{10}$

EXERCISE 23l
(p. 406)

1. a) $\dfrac{2x}{y}$ b) $\dfrac{x-y}{2x}$ c) $x+3$

2. a) $\dfrac{1}{6p}$ b) $x-2$ c) $\dfrac{3y}{2x}$

3. a) $\frac{8}{9}$ b) 7, -2

4. a) $\dfrac{x^2-2x+12}{4x}$ b) $6\frac{1}{2}$

EXERCISE 23m
(p. 406)

1. a) $\dfrac{v}{uw}$ b) $\dfrac{1}{2a-b}$ c) $\dfrac{x}{3-x}$

2. a) $18s^2$ b) $2(x-2)$ c) $\dfrac{2-5x}{x(4x-1)}$

3. a) 4   b) 1, 2

4. a) $\dfrac{x}{6}$ b) 30

CHAPTER 24 Loci and Constructions

EXERCISE 24a Some questions in this exercise have more than one correct solution. Any
(p. 407) reasonable locus should be accepted. Unless stated otherwise, it will always be
assumed that a straight line extends to infinity in both directions.

1. A complete circle

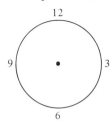

2. One twelfth of a circle

3. An arc from the bowler's hand to the wicket

4. A straight line
(assuming the ground is flat)

5. An arc

6. a) A straight line parallel to the
road at a distance equal to the
radius of the wheel from it

b) An arc at a constant distance
from the curve forming the
bend

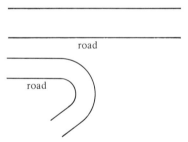

7. A semicircle

8. Approximately a circle

9. A circle (approximately)

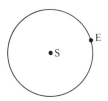

10. A spiral

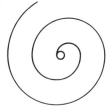

11. a) A circle of radius 80 cm
    b) A semicircle of radius 80 cm
12. A straight line parallel to the top edge and 3 cm from it
13. Two straight lines parallel to AB and distant 3 cm from it
14. a) A circle, centre C, radius 4 cm
    b) A circle, centre C, radius 8 cm
15. The line joining the midpoints of AD and BC
16. The perpendicular bisector of AB
17. The bisector of $A\widehat{B}C$
18. a) The diagonal, BD, of the square
    b) The diagonal, AC, of the square
       Yes. The centre of the square
19. A straight line parallel to AB and CD which is twice as far from AB as it is from CD.
20. a) A circle perpendicular to the plane of the paper with AB as diameter
    b) A circle perpendicular to the plane of the paper with AD as diameter
    c) A circle perpendicular to the plane of the paper with AC as diameter
    d) A circle within the plane of the paper with OA as radius

EXERCISE 24b **1.** A circle, centre O, radius OM
(p. 412)   **2.** The diameter of the circle which is perpendicular to AB
      3. A straight line parallel to AB distant 4 cm from it
      4. A circle on AB as diameter (This assumes that C can be on either side of AB)
      5. A circle, centre A, radius 5 cm
      6. The arc of the unique circle that passes through A, B and any position of C
      7. A straight line parallel to OX, distant 2 cm from it on the same side as A
      8. A circle, centre O, radius OT
      9. a) A quadrant of a circle, centre A, radius AD

b) A quadrant of a circle, centre A, radius AC

10. a)

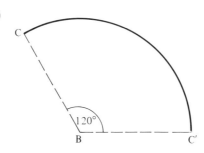

b)

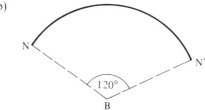

BA turns through 120°

11.

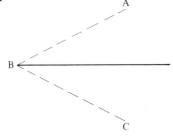

The locus is the bisector of $\widehat{ABC}$

12.

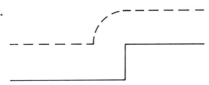

13. a) A circle of radius 4 cm, concentric with the circle of radius 5 cm
    b) A circle of radius 6 cm, concentric with the circle of radius 5 cm
14. The perpendicular bisector of AB
15. It is the midpoint of AC

16.

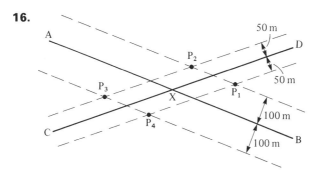

P_1, P_2, P_3, P_4 show the four possible positions for P

17.

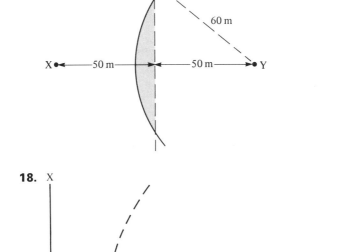

18. X

This curve is called a parabola

EXERCISE 24c Pupils should be reminded of the importance of neat and accurate constructions.
(p. 416) In an ideal diagram the figure asked for, e.g. a quadrilateral, should stand out more strongly than any construction lines that have been used. Sketches should be encouraged for they enable the accurate construction to be well placed on the page and the correct method of construction chosen.

Note that "suitable instruments" can also include a computer with appropriate CAD software.

1.

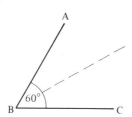

2.

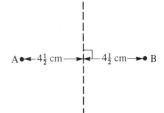

3.

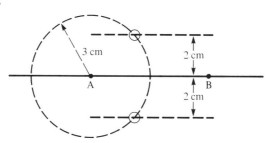

c) The loci intersect in 2 points. 6.1 cm

4.

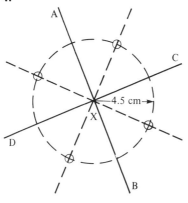

c) Four, 4.5 cm

5.

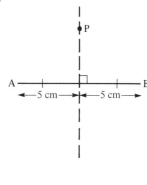

6. The point is equidistant from A, B and C.

7.

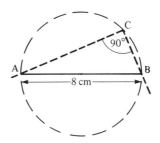

8. 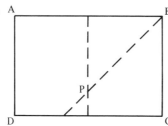 d) PC = 6.3 cm

9. 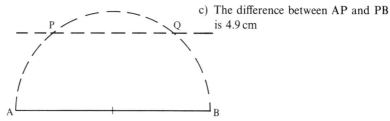 c) The difference between AP and PB is 4.9 cm

10. 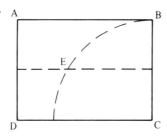 AE = 5.0 cm

11. 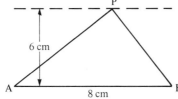 P could also be on the opposite side of AB

12.

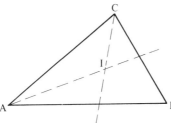

I is equidistant from the three sides AB, BC, CA

13.

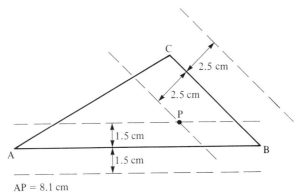

AP = 8.1 cm

14. PB = 4.5 cm

15. CD = 10.3 cm

16. DX = 4.2 cm

17. AD = 7.9 cm

EXERCISE 24d
(p. 420)

1.

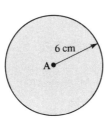

3.

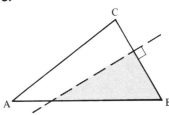

2.

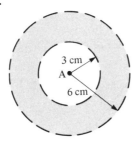

4.

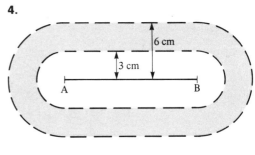

5.

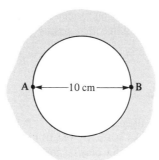

6.

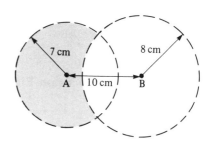

7.

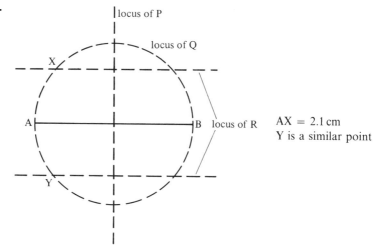

$AX = 2.1$ cm

Y is a similar point

EXERCISE 24e An exercise worth tackling whether it is in your examination syllabus or not.
(p. 421)

1. A sphere, centre A, of radius 6 cm
2. The plane that bisects AB at right angles
3. a) A sphere, centre A, of radius 5 cm
   b) The plane that bisects AB at right angles
   c) A circle of radius 3 cm which lies in the plane that bisects AB at right angles
4. A sphere of radius 15 cm
5. Two circles, one of radius 5 cm and one of radius 15 cm. There are two possible circles in this case but only one in question 4
6. a) A circle, centre D, radius DA
   b) A circle, centre B, radius BA
   c) A circle, centre at N, the foot of the perpendicular from A to DB, radius AN
7. a) Two planes, one on each side of ABCD, each 8 cm from it
   b) The plane that bisects AD at right angles
   c) Two lines, on opposite sides of ABCD, parallel to AB and 8.9 cm ($\sqrt{80}$ cm) from both AB and DC

8. The circle of intersection of the plane which bisects AB at right angles and the sphere, centre C, radius 10 cm (this assumes that the loci intersect)

9. The line, perpendicular to ABC, that passes through the circumcentre of △ABC

CHAPTER 25   Plans and Elevations

This work is useful in making the pupils think about the shape of an object, how it is constructed and how it looks when viewed from different directions. Three-dimensional models are needed. Some may be going on to further study of Design and Technology but even those who are not will benefit.

You may decide that sketching and drawing on squared paper is all that is required and leave the accurate drawing with instruments to the graphics classes.

EXERCISE 25a   **1.** a) None
(p. 424)

b) West elevation

c)

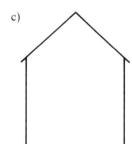

2. a)

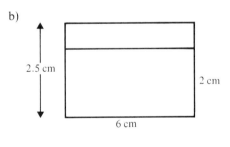

b)

3. a)

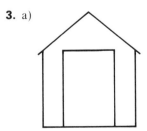

b)

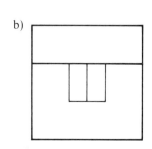

EXERCISE 25b **1.** a) C   b) E   c) G
(p. 428)

2.   **3.**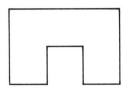

4. a) 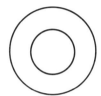   b)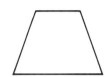

The elevation is the same from any direction

5. It would be a good idea to have a large scale model of this solid.
    a) B   b) E

EXERCISE 25c The diagrams in this exercise and the next are drawn half-size.
(p. 431)

1.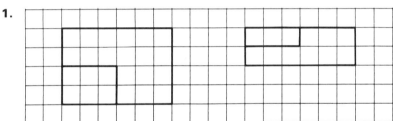

2.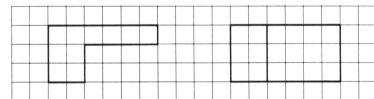

3.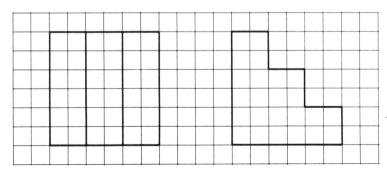

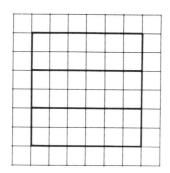

4.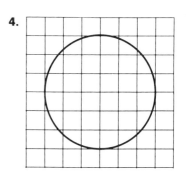

5.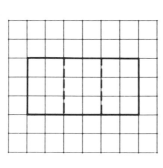

EXERCISE 25d **1.**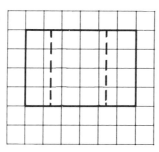
(p. 434)

2.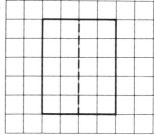

3.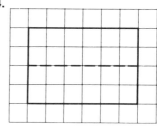

4.

5.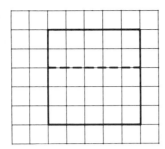

6.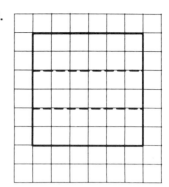

7.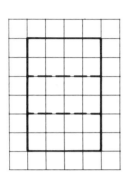

8.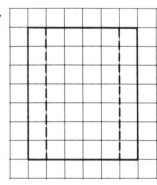

9.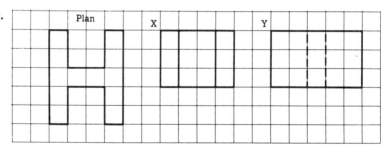

10.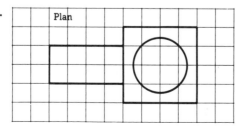

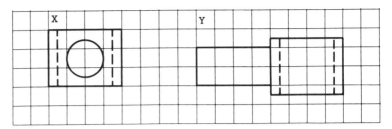

CHAPTER 26   Statistics

Many of the examples and questions given in this chapter involve continuous distributions. The difficulty of dealing rigorously with class boundaries at this early stage is very real. We have followed the principle of using the lowest given value as the starting point for the first group rather than going half a unit below (and above at the top limit). So an age group in which ages from 5 to 9 were given would be $5 \leqslant n < 10$. This presupposes that all the data given (or collected) is rounded *down* to the nearest whole unit below the measured value. We have avoided using $4.5 \leqslant n < 9.5$ on the ground that it is difficult for 3rd year pupils to understand.

This has a knock-on effect when making calculations from the table. In particular the maximum range is affected, but as this can only be an estimate in any case, we regard the method given here to be satisfactory at this stage.

In the answers where bar charts are given, the scales that we have used are roughly half those that the children should use.

EXERCISE 26a Revises the work on bar charts and frequency tables in Books 1A and 2A.
(p. 438)

1.

Pence	0–99	100–199	200–299	300–399	400–499	500–599
Frequency	9	10	16	12	5	4

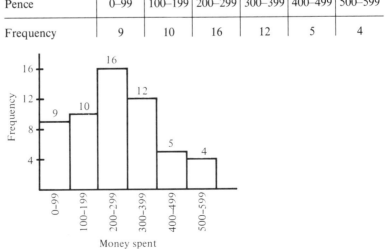

2.

Age (n years)	$7 \leqslant n < 8$	$8 \leqslant n < 9$	$9 \leqslant n < 10$	$10 \leqslant n < 11$	$11 \leqslant n < 12$
Frequency	7	9	11	14	9

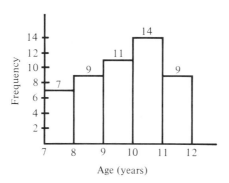

3.

	(Suggested groups)					
Weight (w grams)	$60 \leqslant w < 65$	$65 \leqslant w < 70$	$70 \leqslant w < 75$	$75 \leqslant w < 80$	$80 \leqslant w < 85$	$85 \leqslant w < 90$
Frequency	3	13	6	3	3	2

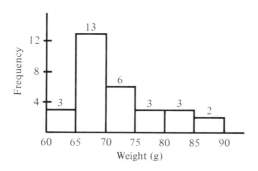

EXERCISE 26b 1.
(p. 440)

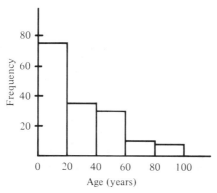

2.

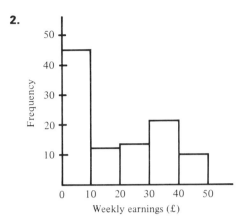

3.

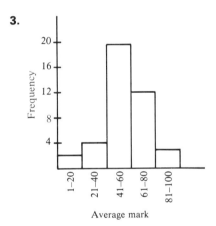

4.

Time (t minutes)	$0 \leqslant t < 10$	$10 \leqslant t < 20$	$20 \leqslant t < 30$	$30 \leqslant t < 40$	$40 \leqslant t < 50$	$50 \leqslant t < 60$
Frequency	8	16	13	9	2	2

5.

No. of hours spent (n hours)	$0 \leqslant n < 1$	$1 \leqslant n < 2$	$2 \leqslant n < 3$	$3 \leqslant n < 4$	$4 \leqslant n < 5$
Frequency	2	12	8	6	2

EXERCISE 26c
(p. 443)

1.

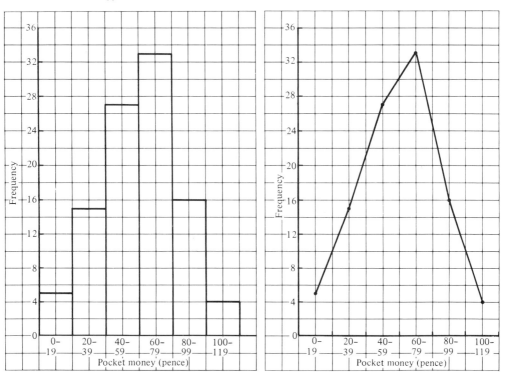

2.

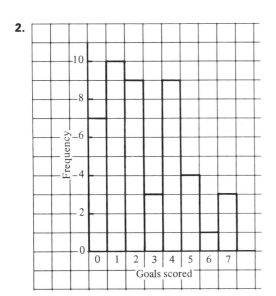

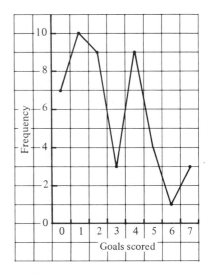

3.

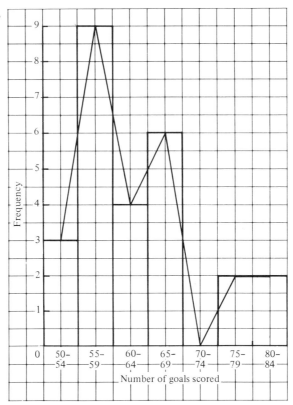

4.

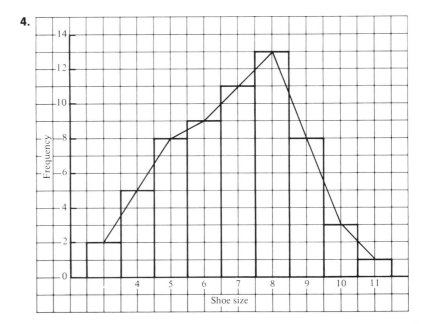

EXERCISE 26d **1.**
(p. 445)

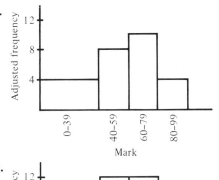

2.

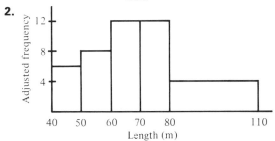

3.

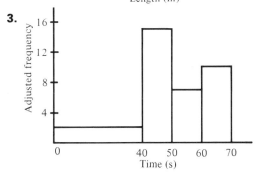

4.

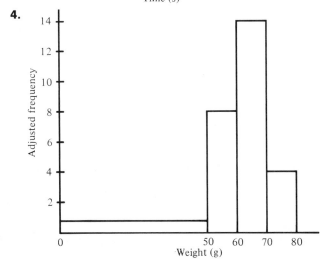

5.

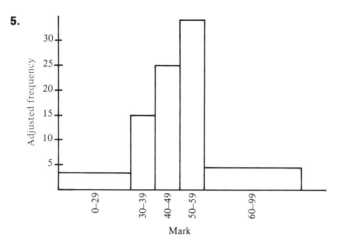

6.

Weight (*w* kg)	$0 \leqslant w < 10$	$10 \leqslant w < 20$	$20 \leqslant w < 30$	$30 \leqslant w < 50$
Frequency	5	10	15	8

7.

Age (*n* yrs)	$0 \leqslant n < 3$	$3 \leqslant n < 4$	$4 \leqslant n < 5$
Frequency	15	15	18

8.

Time (*t* mins)	$0 \leqslant t < 5$	$5 \leqslant t < 15$	$15 \leqslant t < 20$	$20 \leqslant t < 25$
Frequency	10	18	11	6

9.

Height (*h* cm)	$10 \leqslant h < 30$	$30 \leqslant h < 40$	$40 \leqslant h < 50$	$50 \leqslant h < 60$
Frequency	14	11	16	8

EXERCISE 26e
(p. 451)

Revises work on mean, median and mode in Book 2A. Some problems ask for reasons for choosing one or other of these measures and pupils find this surprisingly difficult. As part of their general education, it is worth spending a lot of time discussing the interpretation of statistical measures.

The formula for the median, i.e. the $\dfrac{n+1}{2}$th value, can be deduced from a few examples.

Range is introduced but need not be overemphasised as it is not of any great use in practice.

	Mean	Mode	Median	Range
1.	4.43	2	4	7
2.	9.67	10	9	9
3.	14.1	12, 13, 14	13.5	7
4.	1.84	1.6	1.65	3.7
5.	3.75	4	4	3
6.	8.42	7	8	7
7.	0.725	0.8	0.75	0.4
8.	1.54	1.3, 1.8	1.5	0.7

9. Mean 119.2, median 124
10. Mean £7150, mode £5000, median £5000
11. Mean 180 p, mode 200 p, median 175 p
12. Mean £21.23, median £18.10
13. 17 y, 5 m; 43 y, 9 m
14. 2

EXERCISE 26f
(p. 453)

	Mode	Range
1.	7	13
2.	1	6
3.	5	5

EXERCISE 26g
(p. 455)
1. 4.28   **2.** 3.64   **3.** 1.57   **4.** 120, 2.14

EXERCISE 26h
(p. 456)
1. 5   **2.** (a) 5   (b) $3\frac{1}{2}$ (c) $1\frac{1}{2}$

EXERCISE 26i
(p. 457)

	Modal group	Range
1.	$5 \leqslant t < 10$	20
2.	$28 \leqslant n < 38$	50
3.	36–40	24

EXERCISE 26j
(p. 458)
1. 4.2   **2.** 7.6 cm   **3.** $50\frac{1}{2}$ p

4.

Number of defective screws per box	0–2	3–5	6–8	9–11
Frequency	10	7	2	1

, 3.1

5. 160.4 cm

EXERCISE 26k
(p. 460)
1. 2   **2.** $8\frac{1}{2}$ **3.** 62

EXERCISE 26I **1.** (a)
(p. 460)

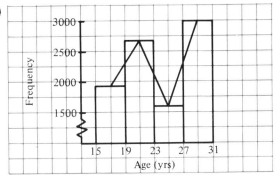

b) 27–31   c) 16   d) 23.27

2. (a)

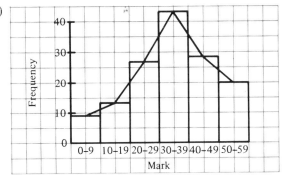

b) 11–15   c) 30   d) 11–15

3. (a)

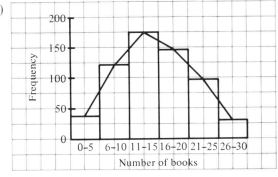

b) 30–39   c) 59   d) 30–39

4. (a)

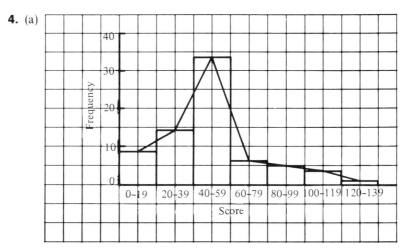

   b) 40–59   c) 139   d) 40–59

5. 45–59; 100; 52
6. (a) 75 p; 75p (b) 90.2 p
7. 21.5
8. 53.5
9. 106.7, 107 cm